Dyslexia an[...]
Useful Tech[...]

D0727702

By E A Draffan.

Published by
The British Dyslexia Association
Unit 8 Bracknell Beeches, Old Bracknell Lane, Bracknell, RG12 7BW

Helpline: 0845 251 9002
Administration: 0845 251 9003
Website: **www.bdadyslexia.org.uk**

Cover design by Dianne Giblin
www.diannegiblin.wordpress.com
Enquiries for Dianne Giblin can be made via **admin@bdadyslexia.org.uk**

ISBN 978-1-872653-61-7

Editorial Note

The views expressed in this book are those of the individual contributors, and do not necessarily represent the policy of the British Dyslexia Association.

The B.D.A. does not endorse the advertisements included in this publication.

Whilst every effort has been made to ensure the accuracy of information given in this handbook, the B.D.A. cannot accept responsibility for the consequences of any errors or omissions in that information.

In certain articles the masculine pronoun is used purely for the sake of convenience.

British Dyslexia Association

978-1-872653-61-7

Published in Great Britain 2012 Copyright © British Dyslexia Association 2012

Printed by Berforts Information Press Ltd, Oxford, UK
www.informationpress.com

Advertising sales by Space Marketing
Tel: 01892-677-740
Fax: 01892-677-743
Email: brians@spacemarketing.co.uk

British Dyslexia Association
Unit 8, Bracknell Beeches, Old Bracknell Lane, Bracknell RG12 7BW

Helpline: 0845-251-9002
Administration: 0845-251-9003
Fax: 0845-251-9005
Website: www.bdadyslexia.org.uk

BDA is a company limited by guarantee,
registered in England No. 1830587

Registered Charity No. 289243

Foreword.

By Robert Bailey.

It is my belief that students flourish best in environments where they feel safe, valued and encouraged. All students, including those with a Specific Learning Difficulty (SpLD) such as dyslexia, can thrive when they are physically calm, emotionally secure and mentally inspired. I have spent more than two decades within specialist SpLD schools working to create such optimal learning environments. Recently, this work has focused on developing independent learning through the use of assistive technologies as a form of scaffolding to support executive functioning.

No two students display identical learning profiles and as such it is seems clear that a one size fits all approach to teaching will not optimise learning. It is important for each student to be accurately assessed, to determine individual needs and preferred learning styles in order to identify and implement a personalised learning strategy. With the continuing growth in technology and its increasingly prominent role in our lives today, it is no surprise that assistive technology forms part of any personalised recommendations.

Margaret Malpas, chair of the British Dyslexia Association (B.D.A.), recognises that all schools should offer multi-sensory teaching, organisational and coping strategies and use assistive technologies as a teaching tool in class.

Maximising the use of assistive technology should be high on any school's agenda if they are serious about leveling the playing field for dyslexic learners. It can make notable differences to pupils with learning difficulties who struggle in the traditional classroom environment.

Edited by E A Draffan, the following chapters chronicle the contributions from members of the BDA's New Technologies Committee and their thoughts on how technology can be used to assist dyslexic learners.

About the contributors.

E. A. Draffan.

E. A. Draffan began as a Speech and Language Therapist spending eight years as the District Speech and Language Therapist at a group of London Hospitals. The work involved supporting disabled people with a wide range of communication difficulties. Having left the National Health Service, she then worked in schools and colleges, specialising in the support of those with Special Needs whilst encouraging the use of assistive technologies (AT). A Winston Churchill Fellowship provided the chance to see how centres of AT were set up in the United States. This resulted in ten years work at the University of Sussex, building and running a regional AT Centre, whilst liaising with others to introduce the concepts of equal access to teaching and learning for those with disabilities. She then went on to work with TechDis and with Professor Paul Blenkhorn and now the University of Southampton.

Neil Cottrell.

Neil Cottrell, 24, is Founder and Director of LexAble, a company that develops assistive software for people with Dyslexia. He was the BDA's Young Achiever of the Year (2010) and Cardiff University's Graduate Entrepreneur of the Year (2011). He is also an honorary research fellow at Cardiff University, conducting research into dyslexia and working memory.

Robert Bailey, BA (Hons), PGCE, MA (Dis), NPQH

Robert Bailey worked as Deputy Headmaster Pastoral at Stanbridge Earls School and has tutored students with Specific Learning Difficulties (SpLDs) for over two decades.

He initiated and directed ATIL as project chair until September 2012, before moving on to the University of Oxford to further study Learning and Technology at Kellogg College. Robert is founder of Technological Tutors Ltd.

Malcolm Litten.

Malcolm Litten recently retired from Mark College as a very special teacher who has spent over 10 years working with students to achieve successful use of speech recognition as well as having a full teaching role. This case study provides an eloquent description of his work.

Contents.

Chapter 1 – An Introduction to Technology.

"If it's right for the dyslexic student, it's right for all students."[1]

Introducing technology to enhance a multisensory learning environment, catering for different learning styles can be the catalyst to a stimulating learning environment for all learners. This is one of the biggest challenges for those who support those with specific learning difficulties including dyslexia. It can be hard to know where to look for the right technology and develop useful strategies. In some cases it can be expensive but even this aspect of accessibility is being challenged with an increase in free and low cost items.

This book aims to help readers explore these ideas further when considering how technology and dyslexia can come together in a mutually supportive way to lead to successful and creative outcomes. Today there is a vast range of technology led strategies that can cater for the needs of most individuals. The software used when thinking about these strategies may be available via mainstream or specialist suppliers, on the Internet or already on your computer, tablet and mobile phone. It may already be on a network in a school, college, university or other organisation. Some of these tools are hidden away, some are underused and some are forgotten. In all cases, supporting agents such as teachers, family, colleagues and carers need to be knowledgeable about their use and management.

---

1   http://bdanewtechnologies.files.wordpress.com/
    2011/01/dyslexia-friendly-schools.pdf

It is the strategies that are developed to incorporate these tools into daily life that are important in the mix of ingredients that contribute to the goal of independence and self efficacy let alone successful learning outcomes. Currently there is concern not only about the literacy levels of school leavers but also about how available and appropriate technology is reaching those students who could most benefit from its use.

> *"The Confederation of British Industry said that too many school leavers struggled to write to the necessary standard, employ basic numeracy or use a computer properly. Almost two-thirds of business leaders also said that teenagers were failing to develop vital skills such as self-management and timekeeping at school. The disclosure – in a survey of 542 firms employing around 1.6m people – will add to growing concerns that the education system is failing to equip children for the demands of university and the workplace."*[2]

The next few chapters aim to encourage more effective and targeted use of those technology resources that are already available in schools and elsewhere to help redress this state of affairs for all students. Computers, tablets and mobile technologies can be considered as creative interactive tools that can enable users with any difficulties or disabilities to develop strategies that will allow them to become more independent learners.

The 'Dyslexia Friendly' environment enables 'good practice' when it:

---

2   http://www.telegraph.co.uk/education/educationnews/9322525/School-leavers-unable-to-function-in-the-workplace.html

- Evaluates and reviews the personal needs of each dyslexic individual, so that suitable support is provided with regular reviews as needs and technologies evolve.
- Ensures **all** those supporting users are aware of user needs and strategies, so they can build on the support over time.
- Ensures those involved in support have access to suitable equipment and training.

How can Technology help?

Technology can provide the necessary risk taking, patient, multi-sensory environment many dyslexic individuals need. This can result in increased confidence and self-esteem, by enabling users to:

- see and hear written text on screen;
- repeat and review information as and when they need to;
- try out actions first and make an informed choice;
- practise skills that meet their needs in both pace and content;
- overcome barriers such as slow typing or writing speed and spelling;
- record and edit ideas easily using ordinary word processing, word banks, predictive and planning tools as well as digital recording and video cameras;
- plan work before starting to write and review output prior to completion;
- demonstrate their knowledge and ability;
- work more independently.

What Technology can help?

Technology for helping those with dyslexia has often been described as 'Assistive Technology' which is defined as "any product or service that maintains or improves the ability of individuals with disabilities or impairments to communicate, learn and live independent, fulfilling and productive lives."[3] At times this has caused a separation in the types of hardware and software that have been considered when supporting dyslexic students – specialist versus mainstream. The mainstream items, such as word processing software packages, tablet apps and mobile phones, may not have specifically designed features to support dyslexia, but they can be particularly powerful in a technology toolkit for dyslexic learners. Many individuals have developed strategies that make best use of their built in features, either thanks to ideas from peers, guidance from tutors or via time spent fiddling along with trial and error.

A range of both mainstream and specialist assistive technologies will be discussed in the following chapters such as:

- Computers with text to speech, speech to text and spell checking.

- Handheld spell checkers, dictionaries and ways of working with word processors to aid writing skills and proofreading.

- Organisational tools including mind mapping and planners.

- Digital pens that scan and read out text or help with note taking.

---

3 http://www.bataonline.org/further-assistive-technology-definition

- Portable technologies to include useful apps for coping strategies.
- Software and apps for improving specific skills in numeracy and literacy.

Why does Technology help those with dyslexia?

Technology in itself cannot make dyslexia disappear with the wave of a wand but it can help. It allows users to work through their strengths to cope with any weaknesses. So programs that offer text to speech allow a user to listen whilst reading the text not just depend on the visual input or have the text highlighted to help with tracking words. Spell checking with text to speech can also help users tell which word they really wanted to use. Typing may be easier than writing and encourage the deciphering of confusing words through the tactile feedback from the keyboard and letter patterns that emerge for example 'were' and 'where' use different finger positions.

Technology does not get cross when you get it wrong and allows for endless trial and error so it is possible to build self-confidence in a way that suits the user. Achieving success in small steps using technology can enhance independence and provide students with strategies that will help them throughout their lives.

This does not mean that technology is always the answer or that difficulties should not be addressed, it is just that the tools when used with effective strategies can encourage learners to tackle subjects in a way that might suit their way of thinking and allow them to progress at their own pace.

Where Technology can help?

Technology based strategies can be used in the home, at school, in the workplace and when on the move. The mobile phone with an alarm call in the morning and task list can act as a reminder for work to be completed later along with the links to the shared mind mapping application with key points to enhance planning and organisational skills. The word processor in the classroom and the social network at home both can encourage literacy skills.

The interactive nature of the technologies now available allows for increased communication between users when connected to the internet. This means that users can be connected from almost anywhere at any time whether by cable, satellite or Wifi. The hardware and software used can be personalised to the extent that speech can be used to input text (speech to text or speech recognition) or text can read aloud (text to speech or TTS) and background colours, fonts and styles can be adapted to suit the user. These are not necessarily special strategies, but can be achieved on many smart phones and portable tablets as well as laptops and computers.

If specific learning difficulties appear to be occurring at school or when studying it can be very helpful to evaluate those areas that are causing problems such as reading, writing and numeracy skills. An assessment can show where difficulties are arising but also show strengths and highlight where technology may be helpful as part of the supporting package of strategies.

Chapter 2 – Assessment and Screening.

The general public is much more aware of dyslexia and related conditions than they were before the internet became so widely available and it is easy to Google dyslexia and find all sorts of checklists and screening suggestions. There is still no totally accepted definitive 'diagnosis' of the condition, but anyone who has problems with reading, writing or spelling is eager to find out whether dyslexia explains their issues.

Traditionally it has been the role of the Educational Psychologist to provide proof that a child or adult has dyslexic learning differences. Especially for the severe dyslexic, this is still the essential route to gain the recognition that provides maximum support in school, college or the workplace. It can take a long time and be costly to follow this route, but there are now on-line and software screening programs that can be used by teachers to obtain some idea of the degree of severity and for milder cases to provide interventions that can provide tools for the dyslexic person to develop strategies to cope with their learning differences.

It is important to remember that screening only highlights factors that are likely indicators of dyslexia and should be thought of as signposts to further investigation and not as an irrefutable diagnosis.

Why screen?

By using a screening tool, the teacher can find out a child's cognitive strengths and weaknesses and from those, deduce the learning differences and the preferred learning style, in order to focus on suitable teaching and learning strategies. There are several levels of screening available:

1. Class-wide screening.

Lucid Rapid[1], and Dyslexia Screener[2] are available for on-line testing as well as on a CD. They are relatively quick and easy tests to help the teacher to find each child's cognitive strengths and weaknesses, their preferred learning styles and to identify any children with more serious problems, who can be followed up with more in-depth screening.

2. Parent-led internet checklist.

There are several checklists on the internet that 'anxious' parents may have found for themselves. Some of these are American and not always helpful for our culture, but where a parent brings in the results from an internet search, it can provide a good starting point for home/school discussion and for planning interventions.

This self-assessment can be 'dangerous', especially for adults if there is no dialogue with professionals to show the way forward, as it can be traumatic to suddenly discover how failure at school might have been avoided.

3. Teacher-led Individual child screening.

This is usually undertaken by the SENCo (Special Educational Needs Co-ordinator) as a result of class screening, where a child is failing to respond to the 'normal learning to read' process or there is a request by a parent. This involves more detailed testing by the SENCo who will interpret the results,

1   www.lucid-research.com/
2   www.gl-assessment.co.uk

but the actual test may be administered by a teaching assistant, who often supervises a follow-up intervention programme. The screening results provide useful evidence to justify a request for a full educational psychologist assessment.

The Lucid programs[3], CoPS (KS1), Junior LASS (KS2), LASS (KS3) and LADS (KS4+) have been developed over many years in the UK and produce good diagnostic results, with some suggestions for follow-up strategies to be found in the manual, but the teacher has to plan materials for an intervention programme.

Lexion[4] was developed and has been used in Swedish schools for 30 years, to investigate the phonological and literacy difficulties that are such an important element of dyslexia and has been translated and normed for use in the UK over the past 10 years. It is not a recognised screen test but it provides a profile of the student's skills and weaknesses. After the test has been completed and analysed, an option is provided for suggested computer exercises relevant to the results. These can be run on the student's computer through a cut down version of the program, MiniLexion.

4. Educational Psychologist Assessment.

This provides a much more detailed analysis needed especially for those with severe or complex dyslexic learning differences. It used to be a pre-requisite for special arrangements for examinations, but tutors and

---

3   http://www.lucid-research.com/
4   http://www.lexion.co.uk

teachers with certain qualifications[5] can now provide assessments that include details about the need for extra time and arrangements such as a scribe and quiet rooms for examinations.

Lucid Exact[6] is a literacy assessment for ages 11 to 24 and designed particularly for assessment for access arrangements for examinations.

5. Student and Adult screening.

For many years screening for adults entering further education and university has been done using several different paper based assessments such as DAST (Dyslexia Adult Screening Test) and DASH (Detailed Assessment of Speed of Handwriting) as well as some networked screening tools. LADS and LADS+ from Lucid have been introduced and in conjunction with the B.D.A., they have developed an online screener 'SPOT your Potential'.

However, an assessment by an Educational Psychologist or a specialist teacher holding a current Assessment Practising Certificate is helpful where a more in-depth analysis of strengths and weaknesses is required. This may also be essential if a Disabled Students' Allowance is being sought[7].

6. Visual stress screening.

Lucid VISS[8] is an easy-to-use computerised Visual Stress Screener to help in the objective identification of people (ages 7 to adult) who are susceptible to visual stress when

---

5   http://www.patoss-dyslexia.org/index.html
6   http://www.lucid-research.com/exact.htm
7   http://www.direct.gov.uk/en/disabledpeople/educationandtraining/highereducation/dg_10034898
8   http://www.lucid-research.com/

reading. Visual stress, which affects 15 to 20% of the population, can affect children's literacy development and is a barrier to efficient and enjoyable reading. Developed over several years of research, Lucid ViSS gives users an indication of the existence and severity of visual stress and predicts those who should benefit from using coloured overlays or tinted lenses to combat the symptoms of visual stress.

TintMy Screen[9] provides a way of testing yourself to see if different coloured screen overlays would help when reading on a computer screen. It is not a test for the various types of visual stress but is an "automated process to determine your optimised screen settings which include font size, brightness level and background screen colour".

A word of caution.

It can be life-changing and even disturbing to discover that you or a family member has dyslexic learning differences. It can be a huge relief to learn from the diagnosis that there are strategies that can help turn skills into strengths that can help areas of weakness, so it is important that you discuss this discovery with professionals who can reassure you and/ or point out the way forward. It is also wise to have a healthy scepticism of screenings by commercial companies that suggest their product is the only solution. There is no 'magic cure' for dyslexia, but there are many different approaches to learning and developing skills that can help you get round the issues as well as ways of coping with daily life.

---

9 http://www.tintmyscreen.com/

Chapter 3 – Strategies for Supporting Writing.

The programs and technology tools to support writing are not like those that support, teach and practise reading, phonics and spelling skills. They are not games and activities but open ended programs that scaffold and support dyslexic students.

Some suggestions mentioned in this chapter are technology tools that enable faster typing or more accurate spelling. Some suggestions are "low tech" solutions that may be all that is required.

Word processing programs have made a major difference for many dyslexic users. They can help with writing in education, work and leisure activities. They can also be helpful for supporting the writing process (getting your ideas organised), and also for those who find presentation or handwriting a problem.

Word processing is a key written communication tool used in schools, colleges and many work situations. It enables easy drafting and editing. Users can move written text around the page easily, using facilities such as delete, cut, copy and paste.

There is no pressure to worry about rewriting texts many times over to achieve a neat piece of writing. Word processed text always looks pleasing. It is particularly helpful in schools, colleges and universities when pupils and students can type longer pieces of work or essays. They are also easier for their teachers to read.

Background colours, fonts (the typed letters), size, colour and style can be changed easily. Underline, bold and italic are simple but effective tools. Often additional features such as borders, clipart and tables, can be added to text.

Some users like to word process, but type very slowly. Using additional wordbanks, grids or predictive programs can help enter text more quickly. Using speech to text or speech/voice recognition can also help as can proof reading with text to speech which will be discussed later. It can be useful to use the same word processing software at home as is used in school or work.

Talking Word Processors and the use of Text to Speech.

Some word processors have a built in speech facility, such as Write:Outloud[1] and Textease[2] to enable users to hear the words and sentences as they are being typed. These programs use synthesised (computer generated) voices to read back text. This can help accuracy and reassure users that the content makes sense. Other software packages support the writing process by acting as an additional toolbar for the word processor program such as TextHelp Read and Write[3] and ClaroRead[4] or WordQ[5]. These toolbars also provide text to speech, word prediction, dictionaries and a host of other features. A simple free Text to speech toolbar with text highlighting for MS Word is called WordTalk[6].

---

1   http://www.inclusive.co.uk
2   http://www.textease.com/
3   http://www.texthelp.com
4   http://www.clarosoftware.com
5   http://www.goqsoftware.com/
6   http://www.wordtalk.org.uk/

Many such programs offer a choice of voices (depending on the program) and some voices are freely available to those in education from the Scottish Heather and Stuart[7] to the English Jess and Jack for post-16[8].

Spellcheckers in Word Processors.

Spellcheckers in word processors can help identify misspellings, or typing errors. However, many computer spellcheckers are not very helpful when suggesting a correction list. They usually suggest words that have the first two letters in the spelling error.

If these letters are wrong it may not suggest the word needed. e.g. type 'sercle' and the suggestions may be 'serial' or 'serve' but not 'circle', although many of the latest spell checkers appear to be improving to the extent that around 70% of errors are caught. However, that still leaves too many errors for most essays and assignments and further help with proofreading may be needed along with the use of text to speech to highlight these 'hard to correct' mistakes. A handheld Spellchecker may be useful. These try to interpret phonic spellings, so typing in 'sercl' will get the suggestion 'circle'.

Write:OutLoud uses the Franklin spellchecking algorithms in the program and many of the specialist programs such as Texthelp Read and Write Gold and Claro Software allows users to add to the database of spell checked words.

Wordprocessing tools such as search and replace however will find repeated errors and correct them. The error (e.g.

---

7   http://www.thescottishvoice.org.uk/Download/
8   http://www.jisctechdis.ac.uk/techdis/technologymatters/TechDisVoices/
    Apply

thay) and corrected version (they) need only be typed once and the other corrections will be done automatically. Microsoft Word has a facility to autocorrect common or personal spelling errors.

This auto correction can be extended by use of a program like Global AutoCorrect[9] that also builds on the user's list of mistakes and works with any text editing whether it is in an email, Word document, Skype message or online.

Predictive programs.

Predictive programs can be used to reduce keystrokes, save typing time and aid spelling. After just one or two keystrokes, these programs try to guess which common or regularly used words the user is trying to type.

It presents the suggestions in a window on the screen, so the user can listen and is then more likely to recognise and select the appropriate word. For example, type the letter 't' and up to 8 or 9 common words are suggested, such as 'the', 'this', 'there', 'they', etc.

Many of these programs also have a speech facility enabling the word processor to talk. Programs such a Penfriend XP[10], Co:Writer[11], TextHelp Read and Write[12] and ClaroRead[13] or WordQ[14] are good examples. Penfriend XP provides prediction and onscreen keyboards with appropriate characters for European languages.

9   http://www.lexable.com
10 http://www.penfriend.biz/
11 http://www.inclusive.co.uk
12 http://www.texthelp.com
13 http://www.clarosoftware.com
14 http://www.goqsoftware.com/

Many predictive programs have additional facilities to make any on-screen text speak not just in word processors. This can be useful to use in other applications, with e-mail and the internet. However, if you type quickly you may want to adjust the settings so the prediction element does not slow you down and the choices are used only when word finding difficulties occur.

Additional Onscreen Wordbanks and Grids.

Some talking word processors have an onscreen wordbank facility, which can save typing time. Wordbanks offer lists of regularly used words or subject vocabulary such as Oska WordBanks[15]. Users select the words they need from the grid and it is entered into the text. Pictures and recorded speech can be added to some wordbanks such as those found in Clicker and Write On Line[16].

As well as simple documents, children can create multimedia talking books using pictures, sounds and even video. Crick software offers many supporting features including text to speech and a pop up grid, direct access to Learning Grids as well as a Picture Library.

Word Banks can save typing time and concerns with spelling as well as support word finding difficulties. Users can listen to the words before selecting the one they need. Users can also create their own personal lists to use in the wordbanks. Teachers can create their own grids of words for an individual student or a specific subject use.

---

15 http://www.clarosoftware.com
16 http://www.cricksoft.com/

Graphic support for text.

Those dyslexic students with strong visualisation skills but possibly severe literacy difficulties, may benefit from using a talking rebus word processor, where words are linked to symbolic representation. The symbols provide good support for preparing and editing work, but can be removed before the final printout. Rebuses can be effective spellcheckers and provide positive feedback for incorrect homonyms. For example Communicate: SymWriter Symbols (**http://www.widgit.com/**), which illustrate the meaning of words, can help clue the reader into the meaning of text as well as support writing skills. This doesn't solve the problem of decoding the text, but it does help the reader to understand what the word means.

Initially, symbols were used to help people who were not able to read or write because of cognitive difficulties. However, in recent years symbols have been used with many groups who have no cognitive problems but still experience difficulty with text.

The **Symbols Inclusion Project** has been exploring how symbols can help many children with reading and comprehension difficulties. Children gain more independence in their learning through having symbols. This has led to significant improvements in motivation and

pyramid, cube dodecahedron equilateral, isosceles, denominator behaviour. For example, there are symbols for all of the maths vocabulary for years 1 to 6. Many children can understand the mathematical concepts but not the language of maths. Symbols help to cut through that. Under this project, a large number of supported learning materials have been made for primary pupils.

There are a number of ways symbols are used:

- Vocabulary lists, providing a printed list of the target words with the symbols beside them.

- Symbol supported reading material or worksheets, including graphic support for new or difficult vocabulary.

- Using symbol software so that the writer can see the meaning of the word typed. This helps especially with homophones and confusable words.

- Visual timetables, clear visual clues to what is happening and what is expected, increasing self-confidence and independence.

- Labels and prompts, simple improvements to the environment to make life that bit easier.

How easy is it to understand symbols?

The majority of symbols are easily recognisible, and require no learning. Other symbols will need to be learned. Widgit Symbols are one of the most commonly used symbol sets. They have a strong schematic structure or set of visual rules, so that a reader can quickly work out what a new symbol might mean.

For example:

| book | library | shop | book shop | librarian | shop assistant |

Other symbols will be understood as the user becomes familiar with the schema.

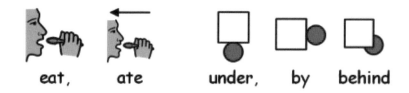

| eat, | ate | under, | by | behind |

And illustrating confusables.

| here | hear | sure | shore | there | their |

When used to support Dyslexia, symbols will usually only be needed for a period of time, acting as a bridge to learning while other strategies can be developed. Importantly they help children engage in learning alongside their peers, and allow them to show their knowledge and understanding independently of their literacy acquisition.

Other methods for inputting text.

It has probably been assumed that when communicating in print most people will be typing and this is a particularly important skill to acquire as early as possible to help with the task of writing. However, there are other methods for inputting text on a screen, such as speech recognition or the use of digital paper and digital pens.

Keyboard Awareness and Typing Skills.

Efficient keyboard skills can be hugely beneficial in education, recording in exams (where permitted) and at work. Correct fingering of keys and the using of both hands should be encouraged at the earliest opportunity. This will discourage the learner from developing the habit of typing with only one hand or slow key pecking with one finger. Such habits can be difficult to break.

As with any skill, regular practice is essential for improvement. Typing skills should be practised little and often; newly acquired skills should be applied whenever the keyboard is used.

A bit like learning a musical instrument, the activities may seem tedious and slow to begin with but successful achievements reap great rewards. Individual users will need plenty of encouragement to persevere. Older users will often complete the whole course, whilst younger learners may need a range of activities, both serious and fun.

There are many programs available to help and encourage keyboard awareness, typing and touch typing skills. Most require loading onto a computer and are used interactively in lessons and activities which monitor progress.

Some programs are "paper based schemes" that can be practised on any QWERTY keyboard.

Some younger dyslexic users find the upper case capital letters hard to identify on a standard keyboard. Lower case key stickers (removable), are available from Inclusive Technology (**http://www.inclusive.co.uk**) to cover the equivalent keys to help overcome this.

Keyboard Awareness programs are usually designed for younger users, to encourage quick key finding through a variety of games and activities. Some are linked to Literacy activities. A low tech alternative is to create key finding games using a Keyboard Mat or try the BBC Dance Mat typing[17]

Good touch typing programs are usually interactive, with full speech support, clear instructions and include sets of graded exercises, starting with the "home keys" (*Home keys are usually the middle letter row and have discreet raised markers on F (left hand) and J (right hand) for the index finger positions) or specific key patterns.

As well as auditory prompts, many include visual options of onscreen keyboards displaying the key required or correct finger positions. Many include drill and practice activities with accuracy and speed scores. Some have reward games to improve speed and accuracy.

Several programs are designed to motivate younger users by setting them in an adventure context, or use a familiar cartoon character and include typing and keyboard skills, as well as games. These usually have scores and reward games to increase motivation and speed.

---

17 **http://www.bbc.co.uk/schools/typing/**

Some recent programs offer a mixture of both standard typing lessons and a choice of activities. Several programs use specific vocabulary lists to combine spelling and typing practise. Others allow users to create their own lists or sentences for practice, that meet specific needs for learning individual spelling patterns or vocabulary.

Some of the portable writing aids, such as the AlphaSmart Neo2 range, have a typing program available for use on their product (e.g. KAZ, Ultra Key). These are available from Iansyst[18]. There are also keyboards that work with tablets and many apps for Apple iOS such as the Ghost Type by Demografix[19] or TypingDroid for older users of the Android tablet[20]

Speech or Voice Recognition Software.

Speech or voice recognition software (sometimes known as speech to text) enables users to speak the words they want to word process. This can be a useful option especially for older pupils, students and adults. Where it proves successful for an individual, there is ample evidence that it can be transformative, enabling communication in print that truly reflects the user's knowledge, understanding and powers of expression. Malcolm Litten's case study in Chapter 9 provides evidence of this fact.

However, it may not be as simple as it sounds. It takes time and a little bit of training. It is not very appropriate for use in the classroom, but can be valuable for producing extended

18 http://www.dyslexic.com
19 http://www.demografix.com.au/
20 http://www.appbrain.com/

pieces of work in a quiet environment or at home. It is important to use a good headset and it can help to have support when first working with speech to text even though applications like Dragon NaturallySpeaking say that minimal training is needed. It is also worth spending a little extra on Dragon NaturallySpeaking Premium edition as that records dictation so that it is possible to listen to what has actually been said alongside the 'read back' function provided by the built-in synthesised voice. This can highlight errors very quickly even though it takes a little time to go over the recording.

Dictation is not always easy when you need to think about what you're going to say and include punctuation. Sentence construction often changes when we are writing text to be read by others and it can help to practice using a digital recorder before dictating directly into the computer. Getting cross, having a cold, forgetting what you want to say and mumbling can lead to unhappy experiences so it is important to try and remain relaxed and enjoy the process.

Dragon NaturallySpeaking comes with its own DragonPad which is rather like Microsoft's WordPad and less complex when compared to Microsoft Word. By using DragonPad you are using less of the computer's resources and may have better results. Microsoft Windows 7 also comes with speech recognition and this works well for most voices but does not have all the features offered in Dragon NaturallySpeaking.

Both the Android tablets and phones and the iPad and iPhone have apps that offer speech recognition when they are connected to the Internet. This means you can dictate

sections of text that can be transferred to message or e-mail systems as well as general word processing.

Digital paper and pens.

In recent years there has been the introduction of digital paper that can be written on using a pen so that the user has a handwritten version of their text but the pen stores the image and synchronises with a computer or tablet using Optical Character Recognition (OCR) and converts the word written to text that is typed. So for those students who prefer to handwrite it is still possible to input text without having to copy type.

The Livescribe Smartpens[21] allow a user to write in note books and on pads using microdot paper that is picked up along with the text by the camera at the tip of the pen. It is possible to print out your own dot paper and with MyScript transcription of the handwriting both text and diagrams can appear on the computer screen. Diagrams, graphs and mathematical symbols are usually kept as pictures.

The Digimemo[22] system uses a slightly different process that allows you to write on any paper and captures the text from its notepad. The same link up with a computer is used to transfer the data so that it appears as a digital document.

MyScript memo[23] does the same with handwriting that has been used on the iPhone, iPod and iPad

---

21 http://www.livescribe.com/
22 http://www.digimemo.net/
23 http://itunes.apple.com/gb/app/myscript-memo/id446368116?mt=8

It should not be forgotten that whilst developing wordprocessing skills and typing in the early stages of a child's education, it is still important to remember physical handwriting. The kinaesthetic action of forming letters into words is very important in providing proprioceptive feedback to the brain, in the early stages of learning to read and write and the development of learning to spell. Some children with dyslexic and dyspraxic learning differences benefit from formal handwriting exercises, where they can concentrate on the process rather than the content.

Handwriting for Windows[24] allows the teacher or carer to generate handwriting practice sheets quickly and easily in a variety of layouts. Once the preferred style has been set up, it can be used to create handwriting sheets of work the child has already created on the computer.

Before writing any essay or assignment it really helps to plan and the next section in this booklet covers some of the software that can be used for this part of communicating in print as well as organising daily life and developing time management coping strategies.

---

24 http://www.kber.co.uk/

Chapter 4 – Planning, Organisation and Time Management Software.

There are so many aspects to planning organisation and time management that it is hard to cover them all in one section of a booklet but very often the planning side for essays and assignments are linked to the use of concept or mind mapping when ideas are generated in a graphical way. Not all dyslexic students enjoy the use of mind mapping some like the structure of lists and outliners such as that used in Microsoft Word with bullet points and numbers but many mapping tools also include this feature.

The problem is there are so many mapping tools so you need to ask a few questions before you make a choice of program. Perhaps it is useful ask about the differences between a concept map and a mind map.

A concept map is a web diagram where each "node" contains an idea, concept or question that is clearly framed with very little chance for ambiguity. These ideas are linked together by branches to show their relationship to each other. It should be noted that concept maps do not always have to take the form of a web – they can be presented as a tree diagram or organisational chart, as an input or output tree or as a flow chart.

Mind mapping is a distinct technique which differs from concept mapping in that short phrases may be used which act as connectors rather than expanding the idea. Mind maps take a particular, prearranged web form. They were developed from psychological theories by Tony Buzan in the 1970s. Combining keywords, images and colour, this highly structured method of concept mapping has become popular with all ages for note taking, brainstorming and creative thinking.

Choosing mapping tools.

Which type of mind map is chosen whether computer based or hand drawn depends on the task, environment, skills, tools available and user preferences – whether there is a preference for a structured or unstructured layout – a map that automatically generates a hierarchy or one that just provides a scattered web of ideas?

For instance if you want to categorise your ideas and you need to apply dates and times or need a timeline you may want to use mind MindView[1], and if you want the complexities of the Gantt chart you might also want to consider Mind Manager[2], MindGenius[3] and iMindMap[4].

However, if you want a simpler look and want to re-order your ideas mainly using a mouse without worrying about a hierarchy Spark Space[5], IMindMap[6] or Inspiration[7] might be the answer. For ease of use consider ClaroIdeas[8] which also works with symbols. All of the programs mentioned allow you to choose from templates for ideas as well as pictures, items from the web and text to speech can be used when editing text. Font changes, coloured background and a different

---

1   http://www.matchware.com
2   http://www.mindjet.com/
3   http://www.mindgenius.com/
4   http://www.thinkbuzan.com/
5   http://www.spark-space.com
6   http://www.thinkbuzan.co.uk/
7   http://www.inspiration.com/
8   http://www.clarosoftware.com

look and feel can be achieved with all the maps so it is not necessary to go with the default view.

For younger users it is important to think carefully about ideas around categorisation and learning to sort ideas before embarking on using computer programs but there are some that can help including Kidspiration[9] and KidsSpark[10].

Research[11] has shown that:

- Mind mapping is a useful technique for organising ideas among more experienced writers. But with children in the younger groups of Years One and Two (five to seven year olds), mind mapping is not a quick and easy panacea. Teachers found it was extremely time consuming for the children to master the technique and even then, it led to only modest improvements in writing for most pupils.

- Prior to the research, there was no real definition of a reluctant writer. The research found that children exhibit a variety of different behaviours and there is no one single cause of reluctant behaviours in writers.

- Although these children were reluctant writers, 95 per cent wrote at home, with or without parental support.

- Pupils made most progress when mind maps were used in conjunction with other visual stimuli such as film and story mapping.

---

9   http://www.inspiration.com/Kidspiration
10 http://www.spark-space.com/index.php?id=kidspark
11 http://www.beds.ac.uk/news/2011/jan/110124-mindmapping

There are mind mapping tools that actually work through the essay planning process such as DraftBuilder[12] and Rationale for older students[13].

There are also many online options where you can share your mind map with other users such as MindMeister [14] and BubblUS[15] or Gliffy[16]. Tablets and iPhones and Android phones can be linked to computer-based mind mapping software and show you the lists you made from the outline of your map or a basic diagram with the main keywords.

Drawing diagrams on small screens and even on larger monitors does not suit all learners. Many mind mapping users still prefer the large A3 sheet with a collection of coloured pens so do download the trial versions of all programs before purchasing as these are available from the websites mentioned.

Uses for mapping software.

There are many different uses for mind or concept mapping programs and a few are suggested in this section.

Brainstorming.

This is an idea generation technique which can be used by an individual or by group. A topic or idea begins the process whether on paper or on computer. Then any ideas, concept, keywords, processes or images relating to the problem or topic are recorded. These form the "nodes" of the map. The

---

12 http://www.donjohnston.com
13 http://www.sightandsound.co.uk
14 http://www.mindmeister.com/
15   https://bubbl.us/
16 http://www.gliffy.com/

relationships between each node, the branches, are then added to start the diagram building process. A hierarchy can be introduced into the map as some ideas may form subsets of others or can be grouped together. As the map is formed it may have additional graphical elements, colour and other cues to help the user retain or reorganise information.

Computer based brainstorming allows for links to be made with many other programs such as word processors which aids organisation of thoughts when writing long pieces of text. Many of the software packages allow for the graphical mode to be exported to other software packages such as word processors.

The results of a brainstorming session can be a concept map which has many uses – it can form the basis of an essay or project, it can produce the solution to your problem, or it can be saved to be used as a revision tool at a later date.

Visual display of information.

Some find the major advantage of concept maps is that they present information visually. Visual thinking is preferred by many people with dyslexia and seeing information graphically can increase both creativity and retention. Images can be used instead of words and tools such as colour; sizing and spatial position can be used to convey information on topics, importance or actions to be taken. Large amounts of information can be stored at many levels but seen as a whole rather than as a mass of text streaming down a page.

Outlining.

Concept mapping programs can be used for outlining documents, presentation or projects. This is possible because the programs contain functions that convert the graphical map view into a text version of the map. Notes functions allow the user to attach text, references or hyperlinks to ideas within the map. Some programs have basic word processing functions in their notes entry boxes, allowing for the addition of lists and tables. Others make an automatic list function from the concept map which can be exported to a word processor. For people with dyslexia, being able to develop a draft version of a document in a visual environment is a great bonus. The entire structure of the document can be seen when exported in a linear fashion and changes can be made at any time.

Multiple applications.

Concept mapping packages can be used in education for lesson planning and presentations and many allow for direct export to PowerPoint or HTML. A project can be planned on the basis of the tasks laid out in Outlook with actions, resources and priorities being assigned to the various branches. The plan can then be exported to a project management tool, word processor or presentation package or held as a reminder or revision tool.

Pros and Cons of computer based maps.

Concept and mind maps have traditionally been created on paper or whiteboards but for the last decade specialist software for creating maps has been available for schools. It is important to consider all aspects of mapping techniques and at all times be aware that this way of working does not suit all those with specific learning difficulties. Here are some comparisons to think about.

Handwritten maps.

- Attractive look and feel but hard to delete errors and can be messy.
- Help to revise content and provide better memory traces.
- Can be created at any time in any place with paper and pencil/crayons.
- Easy to create at any age with any colours and graphics.
- Spelling and writing skills may cause concerns.

Computer based maps.

- Maps can be edited and re-arranged at any time but need to have the tools.
- No limit on the size of the map – your piece of paper is as large or small as you need it.
- Drafting tools such as spell checkers and dictionaries can be used to correct errors.
- Professional images and multi-media files can be integrated into the map.
- Maps can be automatically converted into other formats including linear lists and presentations.
- ICT skills may hamper development of the map.

It is important to appreciate that some mind mappers really enjoy the process of drawing on large pieces of paper with lots of different colours as suggested by Tony Buzan[17]. The enjoyment of drawing and creating a physical picture may be more memorable than the digital version. Either way the process of developing a mind map with keywords can be easily learnt and a useful strategy for not only writing but also note taking and revision.

Organisation for Daily Life.

Organisation is not just about writing it's also about daily life and the use of online calendars such as Google or Outlook within the Microsoft office suite where reminders can be added, appointments can be coloured for importance and synchronisation can occur between tablet, phone and computer. Many apps are also available for making to-do lists and helping with time management.

'Helping Your Child with Organization and Study Skills' from LDOnline[18] is an American website with many useful resources. Making calendars for pinning up on the wall can be part of the process of sorting issues around completing tasks and being on time with everything in place! Later on 'Dyslexia at College' (Editor: John Bradford **http://www.dyslexia-college.com/schedule.html**) has notes on time scheduling with further resources and Hull University have a useful collection of time table templates, articles and mind maps related to organisation and time management for those studying in further or high

---

17 **http://www.tonybuzan.com/**
18 **http://www.ldonline.org/article/5884**

education institutions under their Dyslexia Resources (**http://www2.hull.ac.uk/student/disability.aspx**).

Computer based diary options.

Windows 7 no longer has a built in calendar so you have to have Microsoft Office to make use of the Outlook calendar which can synchronise with Google Calendar as can iCal on the Apple operating system. Both can be adapted to suit your needs with colour changes and various themes. You can set up appointments and add tasks you need to complete with warnings appearing days, hours or minutes before they need to be finished! The Outlook Calendar works in a similar way to iCal on the Apple Mac OS X operating system in that it will sync with mobile technologies using the Exchange server. Using iSync for the Mac, iCal can synchronise your calendar information on your Mac with mobile phones including the iPhone and iPad along with the Google Calendar[19] or there is the free Sunbird calendar from Mozilla[20].

The free alternative from Microsoft is the calendar in Windows Live[21] which also offers synchronization with an on-line calendar and the chance to have many calendars for different uses, linking with Windows Live Mail and Essentials.

Younger users might like to have calendars specially made for them with photos such as those offered by iPhotos from Apple[22] or there are many web sites offering printable

---

19 **http://www.google.com/calendar**
20 **http://www.mozilla.org/projects/calendar/sunbird/**
21 **http://windows.microsoft.com/en-US/windows7/looking-for-windows-calendar**
22 **http://www.apple.com/uk/ilife/print-products.html**

templates for calendars as does Microsoft Word or TextEase which also has a timeline program[23].

Mobile phones as organisers.

Smart phones have taken over the specialist organisers and what were known as Personal Digital Assistants such as the Palm organisers. eXpansys[24] is a website that has good descriptions for many products that have applications or apps to help with time keeping and planning. All the smart phones have alarm systems, notes apps, diary or calendars with appointment reminder systems.

Time management becomes an important part of a student's skill set when it comes to arriving on time, handing in assignments and during exam periods. It is also a part of getting homework done and making the right decisions about when to relax. Scheduling software such as that already mentioned has to be set up to make it useful - you may think you've remembered someone's birthday but there is no point in having a reminder on the day as the card has to be sent days in advance!

Memory support.

There are programs that can help with memory skills such as Cogmed which is a complete online system to help working memory suitable for all ages from pre-school to adult[25]. This was originally developed in USA and there is a complete

23 http://www.textease.com/timeline/
24 http://www.expansys.com/
25 http://www.pearsonclinical.co.uk/Cogmed/Cogmed-Working-Memory-Training.aspx

supporting network with training and chances to trying before signing up.

Jungle memory[26] is another American program accessible online and via subscription. It is designed to help students between the ages of 7-16 years.

Both the above systems can become rather expensive overtime so it may be worth considering the purchase of a one off download program or CD version such as offered by Nessy Brain Booster and Lucid Memory Booster.

Nessy Brain booster[27] is more about study skills for those who are between 13 -18 years of age and learning how a student can help their remembering and revision skills in terms of learning and taking exams.

Lucid Memory Booster[28] designed for children age 4-11 or older. It has a series of games based on an adventure offering plenty of repetition and a chance to build on skills at the user's own speed and ability.

CALSC have developed specialist software that has been available for many years – Timely Reminders[29] for revision and learning to build knowledge in steps prior to examinations. Mastering Memory[30] is suitable for all ages and has memory games that are produced incrementally depending on the user's ability – seeing a few items on the screen then remembering what has flashed up - first just two items and then an increasing number in a shorter time.

26 http://junglememory.com/
27 http://www.nessy.com/brainbooster/
28 http://www.lucid-research.com/memory-booster-description.htm
29 http://www.timelyreminders.co.uk/
30 http://www.masteringmemory.co.uk/

Planning, organisation and time management all depend on memory and it is important to discover where individual strengths and difficulties lie so that the right software is used when thinking of the strategies that might be helpful. Lucid Research has provided a useful explanation of the two main types of memory difficulties encountered by those with dyslexia and how they impact on study skills and daily living:

> *"Usually these difficulties are in auditory working memory, so they tend to forget instructions, have problems learning multiplication tables, and easily lose track of what they are doing (e.g. when reading, writing, or doing arithmetic). Working memory also affects children's acquisition of phonics in school (i.e. learning the relationships between letters and sounds).*

> *Some people with dyslexia have problems with visual memory, so that as children they find it hard to recognise words by sight (e.g. using 'flash cards'), and also cannot find their way around using visual cues (e.g. in an unfamiliar place). Visual memory is also very important in spelling, because a great many English words are irregular and their spelling does not follow phonic rules. The only way to learn to spell irregular words is by using visual memory."* [31]

So it is possible to use applications on phones, tablets, computers and even audio recordings, that have not been mentioned to help with remembering and managing time whether visually with pictures and text or with sound via alarms and voice messages.

---

31 http://www.lucid-research.com/memory-booster-dyslexia.htm

Chapter 5 – Improving basic skills in Literacy.

Introduction.

Acquiring literacy skills is usually the key priority for dyslexic people. Carefully chosen programs can help dyslexic students in all areas of literacy. As well developing spelling and reading skills, such programs have been found to improve learner's confidence [ref: Singleton 2001, R Shoebotham 2010].

The use of technology to support literacy skills can offer opportunities for those with dyslexia to work independently and successfully, in education, work and home environments. Advice and guidance on the types of programs that can help teach and practise reading, spelling and phonic skills are included in this chapter.

Good programs should provide an environment that encourages reluctant readers, allows for user preferences and offers dyslexic individuals the opportunity to succeed. Much of the advice given in this chapter is given for those in schools or tutorial situations and no program can replace a skilled, specialist teacher, but many can offer non-judgemental support and practice on a regular basis as well as being fun.

However, many packages are suitable for providing reinforcement activities at home while some provide home versions specifically for this purpose. Parents and carers should seek the advice from the school or any teachers supporting their child. It is important to choose programs that complement any teaching program and to select an appropriate level of difficulty or specific word list.

Programs for home use should be fun and motivating and should only be done in half hour periods. Be mindful of the danger of over-use and over-enthusiasm with one popular program at home or school. This may eventually have a negative result.

Choosing software.

There are many programs available to support literacy skills. It is important to select these carefully, so they meet the needs of dyslexic users.

Important features and options to consider when choosing literacy programs:

- Spoken instructions and full speech support, with all text on screen read aloud.

- Text that is highlighted as it is spoken.

- Opportunities to listen again or repeat an activity.

- A structured progression or word lists that can be selected to meet the needs of the user in skill based software or predictive tools.

- Spellings, phonics and word lists that are written in lower case, not CAPITAL letters.

- Easy navigable and uncluttered screen with a clear focus on the task.

- Options to record the user's progress can be motivating and helpful to those supporting them .

- A range of user and /or teacher options especially the option to choose the colour of screen backgrounds and fonts.

- Activities that encourage the user and motivate them to continue to learn.

- Activities appropriate to the age range of the learner, particularly for those whose reading ability is lower than their age.

- Make sure any software you choose is suitable for use on your computer or portable technology such as a tablet or mobile phone and that it meets the hardware specifications. For example, some packages will require a CD in a drive to work while all will need speakers or headphones for sound. These small hurdles can create huge barriers in a school environment.

These kinds of programs usually offer a range of games or activities to practise skills in reading high frequency words phonics and spelling. They usually use selected lists or a structured program.

Many programs for children use lists that include words suggested by the National Literacy Strategy (England) and the Letters and Sounds phonics approach used in many Primary Schools.

Many general education packages as well as those that have been developed specifically for dyslexic users can be used to develop and reinforce phonics and spelling skill. In this chapter we will list some packages that are being used successfully. This is only a list of the most popular products as new packages are launched all the time.

Early Phonics Development.

With the drive to deliver synthetic phonics teaching from Foundation Stage there is now a number of early phonic resources that as well as being used with the whole class or small groups, can be used as a multi-sensory tool for those with dyslexia through their use of sound, music and supporting kinaesthetic materials.

Many of the schemes which qualify for the Department for Education's matched funding scheme have associated computer activities. Schemes such as Jolly Phonics, Floppy's Phonics and Yellow Door all have such extras. There are also many free resources on the web. Those in the BBC's Bitesize[1] series are particularly useful.

Several apps for smartphones and other handheld devices can also be found, but beware that many are aimed at the American market and the different sounding phonics and letters will cause confusion.

The company which produces the SUMS software for numeracy (see Chapter 6) has also developed a teaching resource in a similar style for phonics. It is intended for use on a PC with or without an interactive whiteboard for adult led sessions. It has particularly clear sound and screen displays[2].

---

1   http://www.bbc.co.uk/bitesize/ks1/
2   www.sumsphonics.co.uk

Moving on.

Once past letter sounds, there is a wide range of ICT tools that can be used as teaching schemes, tricky areas or specific interventions.

Wordshark 4[3] (Age 5 to 13, PC and MAC).
100s of word lists to use with over 40 motivating games to help reading, phonics, spelling and alphabetical order. The lists include:

- Early years /intervention with the Letters and Sounds lists detailed week by week support for the English Government's synthetic phonic scheme as well as a short phonics course to complement other synthetic phonics schemes.

- Alpha to Omega, Literacy hour and other general course word lists for older users/adults. These include 3 alternative structured courses with 6,000 words including spelling and reading using phonemes, words and sentences.

- 3,000 words and relevant sentences recorded in 13 curriculum subjects for secondary school use.

With such a wide range of lists Wordshark can be used or modified to suit all ages from 5 years to adults. However the simple games interface is more suitable to younger children and pre-teens. There are many user options and the facility to add your own word lists. Detailed records are kept and certain activities can be printed onto worksheets. A new USB version makes it easy to move the program between different computers. Although no specific home user version

---

3 **http://www.wordshark.co.uk/**

is available, it can be used at home to reinforce activities with guidance from teachers.

There is now a reduced version called Phonicshark 4 which focuses on early phonics work and qualifies for the government's matched funding scheme.

Nessy[4] (ages 4 to adult; PC and MAC)(free demo available) The Nessy Learning Programme is an award winning, computer based resource for teaching reading, writing and spelling. Starting at basic phonics and going through to complex writing tasks, Nessy combines game-based learning, teachers resources, animated guides and progress tracking. Nessy Literacy programme can be used as a whole class resource or as a targeted intervention. The built-in "Nuggets" rewards system motivates learners while there is a wide range of printable worksheets and activities for use away from the computer. The package also includes resources about dyslexia that are useful for children to understand their difficulties.

Nessy Games is aimed at home use for reinforcing learning. It uses the same games and word lists and the Literacy Programme. You can add your own wordlists and recordings to both packages. There are also a range of supporting web, iPad and computer packages available from **www.nessy.com** including interactive books, typing and maths resources.

Lexion.(age 4 to 16; PC). (http://www.lexion.co.uk/) This is a wide reaching program that can be used to improve and practise a variety of Literacy and associated skills from early years to 16 years or older. The program has a variety of activities and exercises at a wide range of ability levels

---

4   http://www.nessylearningprogramme.co.uk/

to support phonological awareness, reading, spelling and comprehension. It also includes activities to support Maths, direction and memory. It has an assessment facility that will generate a selection of appropriate activities from the results. All activities come with a range of options in both difficulty settings and personal user settings. Detailed records are kept of all user and their progress.

Catch Up[5].

Designed for primary age users, this motivating program takes the user through a range of exciting worlds to help them achieve reading and spelling 100 high frequency words in CD 1. CD 2 covers similar activities in phonic skills. **Catch Up CD 3** is for ages 8 to 14 years, and the three collections are called The Catch Up Literacy Digital Games.

Progress with Quest[6].

This is a new, fun, highly structured and multi-sensory literacy programme for children aged 5 to 11 years with dyslexia and children who struggle to acquire literacy. Progress With Quest is based on the Orton-Gillingham methods that are well known for teaching children with dyslexia. It has been created by Cheron Macdonald, a Dyslexia Action trained Specialist Teacher and the British Dyslexia Association's 'Teacher of the Year' of 2011.

The programme is structured into 3 sections and takes students on a journey through history- Dinosaur Quest, Ice Age Quest and Stone Age Quest, On completion of all the tasks in each Quest there is a challenge to complete. Once

---

5   http://www.catchup.org/
6   http://www.progresswithquest.com/

achieved children are able to unlock the shield and move onto the next Quest. Children start as Pages and are given tasks and challenges to complete the Quest. The aim is to collect all 3 jewels that are missing from Sir Quests' shield to achieve the title of squire. The programme introduces all the consonants in the alphabet, short vowels, blends, digraphs and high frequency words from the Letters and Sounds Programme to enable successful mastery of early literacy skills.

Xavier Programs[7].

This company has pioneered many programs especially for dyslexic users including:

- **Sounds & Rhymes** – games and activities for vowel and early blending skills.
- **Magic e**; – a game to support the use of silent e.

See also **Sentence Pumper, Suffix** and **Punctuate Plus**.

Acceleread, accelewrite[8].

This scheme was devised many years ago and used the text to speech facilities available on original BBC computers. It was devised by educational psychologists and has stood the test of time, remaining a useful tool despite all the later developments in technology.

The child is presented with a card containing four sentences. Each card contains a particular phonic pattern or number of patterns. The child is allowed to read the card until confident of memorising it. The card is then placed face down and the pupil has to say the sentence to the adult, then type

---

7 http://www.xes.org.uk
8 http://www.dyslexic.com/acceleread

it into the computer. The computer says each word as it is entered, giving audio feedback on misspelt words. It also reads the complete sentence once the full stop has been typed. Mistakes are rectified by the child until the sentence is completed correctly.

Further useful sources of reading, spelling and phonic games and activities include:

- R.E.M.[9]
- Iansyst.[10]
- Sherston.[11]
- Smart Kids.[12]

Software to support reading.

Together with programs that support word recognition and phonic skills, there are popular programs to support reading in the form of electronic or interactive talking books. Interactive reading books span the gap between spelling development programs and talking books (discussed further in Chapter 7). There are many available to choose from, both fiction and non fiction. Some support specific reading schemes others are standalone stories and often have optional activities to support phonics, spelling, comprehension and grammar. Some include story writing activities too.

---

9   http://www.r-e-m.co.uk/
10 http://www.dyslexic.com/
11 http://shop.sherston.com/
12 http://www.smartkidssoftware.com/

Clicker.[13]

Although Clicker is primarily a word processor the range of associated activities that are available for Clicker, and its partner WriteOnLine, make these titles far more useful than that suggests. Owners have access to a huge bank of resources in the form of Clicker Grids and Talking books as well as the facility to design these themselves.

Clicker Phonics is set of 6 CDs to use with **Clicker** that progress from early phonological awareness to simple blending skills. It is designed for younger children but many activities, especially in the more challenging CDs, are suitable for older users up to 10 years. Each activity makes use of sound and visual cues to help develop skills.

Clicker Tales is a series of Early Years CDs that teach literacy through traditional stories that children love. The on-screen books are perfect for a whiteboard as well as individual computers, and there are dozens of activities to go with each story.

Trackers for Clicker is a joint Crick Software and Oxford University Press publication for children aged 7+ who have a reading age of 5+.

The series is based on the outstanding fiction books from Oxford's Trackers structured reading series. It is particularly suitable for struggling readers, reluctant readers, and for English Language Learners.

Find Out & Write About is an award winning non-fiction series that teaches comprehension and independent research

---

13 http://www.cricksoft.com/

skills by presenting carefully graded reading materials with connected writing tasks.

There are also packages to teach French and Spanish, which even adults may find useful! There is also a version of Clicker in the Welsh language.

In short, if you are looking for something to support a young dyslexic learner you would find it hard to find a program more useful than Clicker. Many schools already have the program and there is a home user version available as well.

Rapid Reading[14].

Rapid Reading is an intervention programme with a proven record of success. A full scale, independent study by NFER showed that children using it make twice the normal rate of progress in reading and pupils in Rapid Reading trial schools have trebled their normal rate of reading progress using the programme.

With colourful characters, a dyslexia-friendly font and unique speech-recognition software, Rapid Phonics helps children take the small but important steps they need to make progress in reading.

It consists of a series of interesting booklets which are carefully designed to be age appropriate and attractive. The child initially reads through the book, with the help of an adult. The computer version of the book looks the same as the original and the child can then practise reading it with the help of the included speech recognition software.

---

14 **http://www.pearsonschoolsandfecolleges.co.uk**

The software enables the pupil to practise re-reading the book; prompts and supports the child as they read aloud; provides a simple glossary to identify unfamiliar and difficult words; includes interactive quizzes to check comprehension; records and rewards each child's reading performance.

This successful scheme has now been extended to Rapid Plus which is aimed at Key Stage 3 students with reading ages between 6.6 and 9.6.

Pearson also has other titles in the Rapid range which address Phonics, Writing and Maths.

Useful sources for interactive books include:

- R.E.M.[15] - Search for Interactive books, talking books and ebooks.
- Iansyst.[16] - e.g. Nessy Tales, Spin Out Stories.
- Sherston. [17] - Talking Stories.
- Neptune.[18] - Search for Learner's Library.
- Rising Stars.[19] - Search for ebooks.
- Oxford University Press.[20] - Over 200 free e-books on Oxford Owl.

Some programs are not stories but focus on reading for meaning or specific reading skills. Many are designed to cater for all ages and abilities.

---

15 http://www.r-e-m.co.uk/
16 http://www.dyslexic.com/
17 http://shop.sherston.com/
18 http://www.neptunect.co.uk
19 http://www.risingstars-uk.com/
20 http://www.oxfordowl.co.uk/Reading

Chapter 6 – Improving basic skills in Numeracy.

Literacy has always been the first priority for dyslexic learners but some of the learning difficulties can affect numeracy and maths as well. Maths involves memory, sequencing, direction, vocabulary and problem solving strategies as well as calculations.

Amongst those who are not confident of their ability in maths – and sadly this includes many of those teaching in primary schools - it is common to find that the subject is viewed as a series of unrelated, abstract procedures to be memorised. These are readily forgotten, since they were based on little real understanding. Merely repeating rote procedures may aid memory, but does not lead to understanding, any more than chanting the words of a poem gives any sense of the meaning of the verse. If you feel unsure about something you will begin to feel anxious when asked to do it. Repeated failure produces all sorts of diversionary tactics, from making light of the problem, to bad behaviour and general avoidance of the tasks concerned.

Whilst many people perceive maths, and arithmetic in particular, as series of procedures to be memorized it is far more helpful to approach new ideas as problems to be solved. A method that suits one learner may not be the same as that for another. Problem solving skills are essential in applying basic facts to everyday situations.

Many people's problems with maths arise from lack of understanding of basic concepts. It is important to use concrete materials and discussion to overcome this. Learning basic number facts such as tables can be a particular problem for dyslexic learners yet access to higher levels of maths often depends on this.

Learning styles.

Whilst we still do not know everything about the way in which our brains learn, it is recognised that there are individual preferences for learning methods. Where maths is concerned, there are two poles of learning style.

For example, how would you approach adding up this list of numbers?

$$5 + 6 + 7 + 8 + 9$$

Some people will do this by starting from the left, or from the largest, adding on each of the other numbers in order.

Others will quickly see that the numbers average out, to be the same as 5 x 7. Those who prefer to work methodically from the beginning of a problem to the end and from parts to the whole are said to have a **quantitative** style of learning; whilst those who prefer to seek short cuts or intuitive steps to the answer, are said to have a **qualitative** learning style. More explanation of learning styles can be found in the book *Mathematics for Dyslexics* (Chinn and Ashcroft), who prefer to label the two styles as: **inchworms** and **grasshoppers**.

The quantitative learners will be comfortable with step-by-step methods, working from small stages in sequence, to solve the whole problem. They are often confident with language and verbal expression. Although they may not have the flair and vision for higher level mathematics and may struggle with the spatial aspects of the subject, they may well be able to perform competently at earlier stages of numeracy. They rely on their ability to recall sequential procedures, and will probably feel quite confident in their mathematical ability.

In contrast, the qualitative learners will follow a more holistic approach. They will probably be good at visual and spatial aspects of maths and at recognising patterns and relationships between concepts and procedures. They may be able to *see* the answer to complicated problems, but may not be able to record the steps by which they arrived at their results.

They are more likely to make careless errors than their inchworm peers.

Often most of the early teaching they encounter is based on sequential methods and procedures. This means they may find learning maths difficult, unless they have the confidence to go their own way.

Success in maths requires a combination of both styles of learning, although for each individual, one style will be preferred over the other. Good teaching will involve a mixture of approaches to allow for the different learning styles within the class.

Despite developments in teaching styles and content during the last twenty years or so, the ability to do written sums according to traditional algorithmic methods, still tends to be used as a measure of success in maths. Since there are many teachers who feel insecure in their own grasp of the subject, the security of continuing these tried and tested methods can be attractive. The National Numeracy Strategy tried to address this by encouraging children to discuss various methods of calculation, with a far greater emphasis on mental methods and a general openness to others' views. This approach sometimes foundered when willing adults tried to impose their methods on children who asked for help. It also arrived too late for many of those whose feelings of failure were well established.

What sort of problems do dyslexic learners face in the subject?

It is common to find dyslexic learners have strengths in the right-brained areas, which often correspond with the qualitative learning style. However the nature of each individual's learning difference, as I would prefer to call it, means that there is no simple description to suit all.

Some problem areas that may affect the dyslexic learner are:

- memory problems making it difficult to recall basic facts or carry out mental calculations involving several stages.

- slow processing speed - practice with basic skills helps to consolidate learning but a slower dyslexic student will actually get less practice than his faster peers, even though he probably needs more practice to consolidate his skills.

- orientation and sequencing difficulties.

- problems with visual perception which lead to confusion over symbols such as + and x, etc.

- anxiety - this seems to affect those who find difficulty with maths far more than those who find difficulty with literacy

- difficulty with mathematical language.

- the pupil's mathematical learning style does not match the teaching style being used.

- There is much more to maths than numeracy but, since the early stages concentrate on number work, this tends to set learners' attitudes to the whole subject. It is also frustrating to note that many pupils with good mathematical understanding are prevented from accessing teaching groups working at higher mathematical levels, where they may well be successful, because they have not scored well on written tests of basic arithmetic.

Computer programs can be useful for practice of basic skills and for developing problem solving. As with assistive technology for literacy, users need to be taught how to use tools such as a calculator efficiently. Teachers also need to realise that a calculator can be a useful teaching tool and not just an excuse to avoid mental arithmetic.

How can technology help?

When used to practise basic skills, computers can give immediate feedback, without the criticism or judgement, which may arise in the classroom. Good programs can be adjusted to suit the individual's level of knowledge and speed of work. As with board and card games, the programs themselves cannot be universally useful, without some management and discussion of their use and of the strategies involved in solving problems. Shutting a child away in his/ her bedroom with a selection of the software mentioned in this booklet, will not produce a happy and confident mathematician !

There is a wide range of software on the market with associated claims for its efficacy. Likewise there are now many free activities available on websites. Some of the purchased software is now available via the web on a subscription basis whilst other items have reduced prices for home use. Similarly, there is a range of people seeking advice over what to buy. Software that fits well into a short burst of computer activity in the classroom for an individual or a small group will not always be appropriate for home use, where there is more time for individual access.

1. Calculators.

Calculators are the most obvious and useful pieces of technology for numeracy. Their use attracts two poles of reaction. On one hand are those who see their value in investigating numbers and demonstrating mathematical concepts. Others argue that they have no place at primary level as they will undermine the development of mental arithmetic skills.

Now that calculators are readily available and affordable, the latter opinion can seem like trying to un-invent the wheel. As with so many of the rapidly developing technological tools nowadays, surely it is better to harness their power and use it effectively than pretend they do not exist?

Various opinions have been expressed in official documents.

The Cockroft Report into the teaching on mathematics (1982) acknowledged the issue of fluency in mental and written calculations and the use of calculators and advised that:

'the availability of a calculator in no way reduces the need for mathematical understanding on the part of the person who is using it.'

and that:

'the weight of evidence is strong that the use of calculators has not produced any adverse effect on basic computational ability.'

More recently, from Ofsted's report on the Teaching of calculation in primary schools (15 Apr 2002)[1]

To improve the quality of teaching and pupils' standards of attainment, schools need to:

- o *teach pupils to judge when it is sensible to use mental, written and calculator methods, to choose the appropriate method or combination of methods, and to apply these accordingly.*
- o *encourage pupils' use of mental strategies, such as rounding, to check an answer when using a calculator.*
- o *continue to look for ways to make use of the calculator as an effective teaching and learning tool.*

Like other technological resources, children do need to be taught how to use a calculator efficiently. They do allow real values to be used in problems but the speed of calculation means that skills of estimation, to check that answers are sensible, become even more important.

---

1 http://www.ofsted.gov.uk/resources/teaching-of-calculation-primary-schools

There are some examples of talking calculators, which read out the numbers as they are entered, which may be helpful to dyslexic users and others who are prone to mis-entering values. Some computer based versions also display the various stages of working, which is very helpful for checking purposes if a final answer seems unreasonable.

2. Creative computing solutions.

It is often said that one truly grasps a concept by explaining it to others. Now that there is ready access to multimedia authoring tools, especially on iPads with apps such as Explain Everything, iBook Creator and similar products, it can be very useful to encourage learners to produce something or give some sort of presentation to explain a process or concept to others. This creative process may be especially suitable for those dyslexic users who have particular artistic strengths and as narration can be recorded rather than typed. Working collaboratively is an excellent way overcome problems by discussion with others in the group.

Spreadsheets are a basic tool in computer software. They have many uses in maths, notably in problem solving from basic money management to solving complicated equations.

3. Software to reinforce and give practice in basic numeracy.

The most common way in which software can be used to help learners, is in providing further reinforcement and practice of the skills they have encountered in class. In many cases the practice drills will be set in the context of some sort of game, possibly with points awarded for another game, as a reward for success.

There are many titles available on the various platforms nowadays. Some schools have invested in online resources which pupils are expected to use. Often these have a timed and competitive element, which can be discouraging to those less confident in the subject. We do not value speed ahead of accuracy when it comes to literacy skills, yet undue time pressure is sometimes exerted over numeracy skills.

When planning to help a pupil at home, it is important to be aware of any computer based resources used in school from discussions with teachers. It can be more useful to have contrasting activities for home use, especially if the child is finding those at school not particularly helpful.

With so much now available online, as free activities or on sale as free standing tools it is impossible to cover everything. These are a few suggestions that have been found to be particularly useful.

Numbershark 4[2] (Age 5 to 16 years).
Numbershark is by the makers of Wordshark and has the same type of colourful, fun graphics in structured learning tasks and a similar range of enjoyable reward games. It covers number recognition, sorting, the four main rules of numbers, i.e. addition, subtraction, multiplication and division as well as decimals, fractions and percentages.

It gives users the chance to build up confidence, and the opportunity to practise those aspects of numbers that worry them, in an enjoyable way. Study of the manual by the supervising adult is essential as there are so many options.

---

2   http://www.numbershark.co.uk

Dynamo Maths.[3]
A Three Stage On-line programme to develop Number Sense and Numeracy Proficiency, Dynamo Maths has been developed through extensive research and with the support of Dyscalculia practitioners. It gives children a strong foundation for the early development of Number Sense.

Dynamo Maths tackles early maths skills such as: Patterns, Bonds of 10, Number facts, Shape and Space, Place Value, Telling the time, Money Fractions, Pictograms etc. The programme addresses over 20 Dyscalculia difficulties such as: Subitising Auditory Memory, Number Recall, One-to-one correspondence, Visual Memory, Sequencing, etc and is ideal for supporting and boosting the confidence of children who are struggling with maths or are dyscalculic.

The programme has personalisation features that allow the Teacher or Parent to target and track students progress, select activities for individual children and set on-line homework that is marked, scored and tracked.

Multi-Step Maths[4] is a similar resource covering the primary school curriculum for ages 5 to 11.

SUMS[5].
This expanding set of simple reinforcement games covering the national curriculum for Maths has proved very popular and effective in many schools and offers exceptional value for money. One advantage of SUMS is that the games run on various small hand-held devices as well as traditional computers. The instructions are not spoken but the graphics

3   http://www.dynamomaths.co.uk
4   http://www.multistepmaths.co.uk
5   http://www.sums.co.uk

are generally so clear and simple that this should not present a problem. Many examples of the games are available as free examples on their website.

MathBase[6].

MathBase was originally created to help secondary pupils who for a variety of reasons were experiencing difficulties in maths. Because of its simple and effective approach it soon became popular in primary schools. In addition, MathBase can also be helpful for adults with a previous fear or dislike of maths who need lots of basic practice.

The software is colourful and well laid out but not age specific. The material is mainly presented in the form of a simple matching game with distracting or superfluous content removed.

The software presents the material in a series of manageable small steps which users can take at their own speed. The aim is to boost the learner's confidence in fundamental number and number operations. Progress in maths is obviously harder without this basic confidence.

The software is effective as an additional resource when used in conjunction with other materials. It is easy to use and does not need complex explanations. MathBase is remarkably inclusive and can benefit both very able students, those with a high degree of special educational need and those in between.

MathBase is used in more than 2000 UK schools, including 250 special schools. Many primary schools use it from year

---

6   http://www.mathbase.co.uk

1 to year 6 inclusively with pupils of mainstream ability and those with SEN.

MathBase runs natively on Microsoft Windows systems. It does not operate on Mac systems without the use of special software. MathBase can be loaded on to a central server or deployed to individual machines. No data storage is undertaken.

Number Gym[7].

The Number Gym won the 2007 Pirelli Internet Award for the Communication of Mathematics "for its ability to provide children, by means of interactive tools and games, with an informal and fun approach to the complex world of mathematics" The activities cover all Key Stages and the associated table and number bond trainers provide excellent practice. There are sample versions available on line and special rates for home and tutor use.

MathMania[8] (Age 7 to 14 years).

Navigate through a maze finding a key and reaching the exit with the required score. Score points by collecting gold bars or by answering questions to get through barriers. Once each maze is completed, a puzzle appears and then another maze. There are four levels of difficulty for the questions, which can be set on number, time, measurement, shape and space or a mixture of all these in a lucky dip.

It is possible for teachers to edit the question bank. Pupils enjoy this program as it is simple to use and fits well into a

7   http://www.numbergym.co.uk
8   http://www.topologika.co.uk

short lesson. The questions vary from simple sums like 5 + 8 to different equivalents in words.

The latter is most useful as this is an area which causes great problems in maths. MathMania is simple and effective and good value.

Topologika also have other useful programs such as **Talking Clocks Plus** which covers reading the time on both digital and analogue clocks: a task which can be difficult for some dyslexic learners.

ConquerMaths.[9].

ConquerMaths is a tutoring resource for maths which is available on-line by subscription to home or schools users of all ages. It has over 1000 animated and narrated maths lessons. There are also some diagnostic tests to identify particular difficulties. It is also possible to purchase some lessons e.g those for Key Stage 3 and 4 as separate CDs.

To use the program you need to ...

1. Watch and listen to short tutorials (2 to 10 mins) explaining the principles of that lesson in simple steps and using worked examples. You can stop and rewind any time you want to go over something again.

2. Then test yourself by completing the online worksheet. It is best to do your working out using pencil and paper. You can print out the worksheet and work as you would in class and then enter your results on the computer for checking.

---

9   http://www.conquermaths.com

3. Finally, view the worked solutions, which will guide you through your working out and help you to understand any areas where you went wrong.

Each lesson also has a summary sheet which can be printed out as a reminder or for revision.

4. Problem solving.

These programs are most valuable if used collaboratively so that strategies can be discussed and developed. They therefore provide an excellent way for parents or others to support learners.

Maths Circus Acts[10] 3, 4 and 5 (Age 5 to 14 years).

The endearing puzzles in Maths Circus have been available for many years and yet they still provide an entertaining challenge. Twelve different games can be played and each one has five levels of difficulty. All the puzzles require reasoning skills. There are straightforward instructions. The colourful graphics relate to circus life with seals, lions, high wire acts etc. The early levels can be solved by trial and error but learners gain the greatest benefit if they verbalise their reasons for following a procedure to solve a puzzle. For teachers there is also a useful set of 24 activity sheets which can be photocopied.

Zoombinis[11] Adventures (Age 7 to 14 years).

Zoombinis are delightful little creatures with different feet, eyes, heads and noses. In their adventures they have to be guided through different obstacles and challenges. This needs careful observation, trial and error and logic reasoning.

10 http://www.4mation.co.uk
11 http://www.amazon.co.uk/Zoombinis-Characters-Software/
    b?ie=UTF8&node=777118

The programs are very well presented with superb sound and animated effects and are very enjoyable.

Users will gradually gain confidence and learn the importance of working logically as they use these programs. Once again collaborative working and discussion of tactics is really valuable. The triple pack is available from Amazon for around £20.

5. Other resources.

Traditional board and card games are still very valuable in developing the strategic thinking necessary for success in maths. Examples of technological versions can now be found in the various Brain Training packages for games devices such as Nintendos. There are also many adventure games and puzzles which require logical thought and problem solving.

Finally.

In our country there is justifiable concern over standards of numeracy amongst all ages. Having been strong in the areas of Science, Technology, Engineering and Mathematics in the past we now lag behind other countries. Young children enjoy their early experiences of number yet, as they progress through our education system this enjoyment seems to turn to anxiety and, for some, real panic.

Mahesh Sharma, a world renowned expert in the remediation of mathematical skills, refers to a condition he calls Mathephobia …

> *"Some people believe that the early settlers brought this disease with them although the disease was not recognised*

as such. Many people are carriers but escape the usual medical checkups.

A mother or father with Mathephobia may inadvertently pass it on to their children by their negative attitude towards mathematics."

Too often adults report that they have felt intimidated in maths lessons and have been too embarrassed to ask for help when they have not understood a task. This can easily apply to those with specific learning differences. Technology can be helpful, especially now that truly multimedia resources which use sound and visual images together are readily available. However attitudes towards the STEM subjects in our education system and in general society need to change if we are to raise standards for the future.

Chapter 7 – Accessing Information and the curriculum.

This chapter may appear to overlap with some of the others that you have read, but it aims to cover some of the strategies that can be used to overcome difficulties that may arise when trying to gather information or access the curriculum.

In recent years we have all been overwhelmed by the amount of data that we can access via the Internet, through television, radio and through print. The increase in 'stuff' has mainly come from the Internet and it is now a shared experience. It is no longer just the experts that write on the web, because we can all add our own knowledge without any specialist training in HyperText Markup Language (HTML) or java script etc – examples of coding languages used to develop web pages. This freeing up of the interactive side of the web has been achieved with a series of templates and text editors all looking like a computer based word processors. We can upload images, video and audio, share comments and have conversations about our favourite topics. **YouTube** and **Facebook** have become household names.

So it is not just the experts who are providing us with support, many parents and teachers have written their own articles in blogs or answered queries in forums. There are social networks with groups that have grown up around topics such as Facebook and the government is keen for us to download their information rather than calling for help.

Unfortunately not everything that is digital is accessible. In other words despite the fact that more information is being presented in different ways (for example- there are videos on an ever increasing range of topics from showing you how to use computer programs to grooming your pet and there are audio books of some of the best novels) it is still rare to find textbooks available as audio books or e-books and all too often the document you want to download cannot be used with text-to-speech. It is also important to appreciate the skills and abilities required to use the technologies that enable those who have reading difficulties to make the most of the huge variety of web-based content.

As has been discussed, there are some easy to use assistive technologies with simple menus, font and colour changes plus text to speech. However, there are times when these tools fail to fulfil the needs of dyslexic students accessing complex materials provided as part of the curriculum. Not all mathematical symbols can be read aloud, some documents have text that is like an image and if you drag your mouse across it you will find you cannot highlight the text. This usually means it cannot be read unless you use something like TextHelp Read and Write Screenshot Reader[1] or Abbyy FineReader[2] which does an instant scan of the selected part of the inaccessible content and converts it into readable text.

The following sections aim to provide you with more information about alternative formats and electronic reading devices, apps and e-books, reading and scanning pens and strategies for reading text on the web because, although the web offers a multimedia, experience much of the content and the interactions that take place are text based.

---

1   http://www.texthelp.com/uk/our-products/readwrite/features-pc/reading
2   http://finereader.abbyy.com/professional/full_feature_list/

Alternative formats.

Textbooks and work sheets are the main ways that students have for accessing text in the classroom if they are not reading from a board or projector. Trying to keep up with the page turning of one's peers, if reading is difficult, can be very demoralising. Several government projects have shown that the introduction of alternative formats for the text provided to students and the use of assistive technologies, such as text to speech plus changing the look and feel of a document, can help with reading and writing as well as increase confidence levels. [3] The Load2Learn[4] project in England has introduced the chance for teachers to provide accessible texts and Call Scotland have also been providing Books for All [5]as a means of expanding the number of textbooks available in Word or PDF format (that can be read using assistive technologies) to students with print impairment including dyslexia.

However, it is possible to produce worksheets and ebooks at home in an accessible way. Just using your own word processing software with the help of the many guidance articles on the web and YouTube is one method but there are programs like iBook Author[6] or ones that take your blogs or webpages and convert them into a single publication such as Zinepal[7].

Whilst making these worksheets and ebooks it is important to be aware that everyone has their own preferences for the way text is presented – allow users to change the way

3   http://www.altformat.org/mytextbook/
4   http://load2learn.org.uk/
5   http://www.books4all.org.uk/Home/
6   http://www.apple.com/ibooks-author/
7   http://www.zinepal.com/how

your creation looks and enable text to speech. However, if you are working with a child using text to speech they may find the process quite tiring and work more slowly than their peers. Some children find the synthetic voices distract them and they prefer just text highlighting or changing the presentation of the text. By providing an accessible digital version of a worksheet this can be achieved and it is possible to enlarge the fonts, change the style, add coloured backgrounds and increase line spacing to name just a few of the options. All this can be achieved in most word processors or via the use of the technologies mentioned in Chapter 6.

The BDA has provided a style guide,[8] which includes some pointers that may help to make a document text to speech and reader friendly:

- Put full stops after headings to make the voice drop and pause; a pale tint similar to the background colour will make the dots less visually distracting.

- Put semi-colons, commas, or full stops after bullet points to make a pause.

- Use Styles in Word to organise headings and formatting.

- Keep automatic numbering to a minimum as some text readers will not read these - this will affect the next piece of advice if you are numbering chapters or sections so be aware of this issue and **test your work with various text to speech applications if possible**.

- Contents Page listings should be hyperlinked to the relevant section to aid navigation. Number menu items.

---

8   http://www.bdadyslexia.org.uk/about-dyslexia/further-information/dyslexia-style-guide.html

- Use internal and external hyperlinks for ease of navigation.
- Avoid text in capital letters in mid-line, as they may be read as single letters.
- Include as few signs and symbols as are absolutely necessary, e.g. asterisks or dashes (both short and long), as these will be spoken.
- Long dashes should be avoided: use colons to make the voice pause.
- Use straight quotation marks. Curly or slanting ones may be read out as 'back quote' by some screen readers.
- Avoid Roman Numerals and No. for number.
- Consider whether abbreviations and acronyms need full stops.
- Text readers may have difficulty with tables in Word and may not automatically move on to the next cell without manual use of the Tab key.
- Avoid text in images. Listeners cannot hear it. It can help to explain the image in the main text if that is not part of a test question.
- Use hyphens in compound words to aid text reading pronunciation.
- Chunk phone numbers to avoid being read as millions or hundreds of thousands.

If worksheets of documents have been produced in a way that does not allow for reading aloud, such as a PDF that cannot be read with Adobe Reader using Read Out Loud[9] or

---

9 **http://help.adobe.com/en_US/Reader/8.0/help.html?content=WS58a04a8 22e3e50102bd615109794195ff-7d15.html**

other text to speech programs such as TextHelp Read and Write, Dolphin SaySo or ClaroRead ,then it is possible to convert the documents using online services such as Calibre[10] or free downloadable programs such as Webbie Accessible PDF Reader[11]. Students who have a Disabled Students Allowance may like to try 'Access My Studies'[12] which offers online conversions with the use of ClaroSoftware. But it should be noted that these options will change the look and feel of the document and even strip out the pictures in some cases, so it is important to check what is needed in each situation.

Capturing documents and reading them in apps on the mobile phone or tablet is also possible using such apps as CapturaTalk[13] on Android and ClaroSpeak[14] on iOS devices such as the iPhone and iPad. ClaroSpeak does not convert documents in the way CapturaTalk works so an extra app such as Image to Text [15]or PDF to Text[16] is needed before you can copy the text into ClaroSpeak to have it read aloud. The other option is to use an ebook app which works with Talkback[17] on Android or VoiceOver Speak Selection[18] on the iPhone or iPad.

10 http://calibre-ebook.com/about
11 http://www.webbie.org.uk/accessiblepdf/index.htm
12 http://www.accessmystudies.com/
13 http://www.capturatalk.com/
14 http://www.claro-apps.com/clarospeak/index.html
15 http://itunes.apple.com/us/app/image-to-text-ocr/id431757093?mt=8
16 http://itunes.apple.com/us/app/pdf-to-text/id432054682?mt=12
17 https://play.google.com/store/apps/details?id=com.google.android.marvin.talkback&hl=en
18 http://www.apple.com/accessibility/iphone/vision.html

Ebook Reading.

One tends to think of the popular Kindle[19] reader as the main e-reading device seen on trains and whilst waiting for a bus, but in fact tablets such as the iPad and Samsung Android or Toshiba Windows tablets can be used for e-reading and there are also Sony[20] and Kobo[21] readers. All are beginning to go for coloured backgrounds with varying degrees of resolution, but the main difference is that dedicated e-readers tend to use e-ink electronic paper as opposed to the back-lit screens found on tablets. This can be a bonus as it reduces glare and allows you to read outside.

The e-reading devices tend to be linked to particular libraries of books such as Amazon (Kindle), WH Smith (Kobo) or The Reader store (Sony) but all can load books and documents via a computer or other areas on the web. The PC, tablet and mobile phone apps that have the same name will also link to these book stores and can once again take in other documents as long as they are saved in the correct format.

An e-book market place such as Amazon may only offer books in its own format such as .azw[22] (that is the e-book file ending) and other bookstores offer epub or iBook. So when choosing an e-book reading device you need to be aware of the type of books you want to read as well as the way they are presented on the app. The problem is compounded by the fact that there are so many apps available for computers and tablets and these all come with different accessibility options for the various formats. Not

19 https://kindle.amazon.com/
20 http://www.sony.co.uk/hub/ebook-reader
21 http://www.whsmith.co.uk/koboereaders.aspx
22 http://en.wikipedia.org/wiki/Amazon_Kindle

all offer text to speech and there may be copyright issues that prevent it being enabled where it is available, but all offer some font changes and background colour options. Blio[23] comes with extra voices and will read most e-books. It allows you to import your own books in PDF, EPUB, or XPS format. iBooks[24] on the iPhone and iPad will work with VoiceOver and also takes in PDF and EPUB. Moon+ Reader for Android also allows for annotations, highlights and bookmarks. Most e-reading apps now offer a few font size options and a chance to change the background colours. For example Kobo, Stanza and Reader for Sony available for Windows, Apple, Android and iOS (iPhone and iPad). It is worth searching on the various app sites for more details about the e-book reading apps such as the Apple app store (**http://www.apple.com/uk/iphone/from-the-app-store/**), the Google Play Store (**https://play.google.com/store/apps**) and the Windows app store (**http://www.windowsphone. com/en-GB/marketplace**).

There are also highly interactive children's talking books which have human narration with lovely pictures such as those offered for younger children by Nosy Crow Ltd[25]. The vBookz iPad app has narration for a wide selection of classic books using synthetic voices (text to speech) with a magnifier to see where you are in the book. [26] Some websites such as StoryNory [27] make it possible to listen (British English human narration) and read chapters from books online as well as

---

23 **http://www.blio.com**
24 **http://itunes.apple.com/gb/app/ibooks/id364709193?mt=8**
25 **http://nosycrow.com/**
26 **http://www.vbookz.com**
27 **http://storynory.com/**

offering them as a free weekly subscription through iTunes or via email.

Pros and cons of reading on tablets.

Pros	Cons
Light and fast boot up	Audio poor in classroom
Can offer font changes and text to speech	Desktop software tends to do more within one program
Build a personalised toolkit	? multitasking
Many options for similar strategies	May not be able to combine such things as TTS, text highlighting, font and line changes as well as annotations.
Long lasting battery for reading at will.	Have to remember to sync with one computer and not all apps accept accessible formats

Reading and Scanning Pens.

These pens offer a portable solution for supporting reading rather than reading a whole book and work with paper based information where words can be read aloud and defined via the pen's dictionary or scanned and stored for use on the computer at a later date.

The Reading Pens[28] with their Oxford Dictionaries and text to speech are held rather like an ordinary fat pen and drawn across the text to enable the recognition to occur. Words are read aloud and ear buds are provided, so that the user hears the pronunciation and can check the meaning in the dictionary. Whole lines of text can be transferred to the computer so this can be very useful when working with books that are not available online or other documents when quotes are needed if you are a student writing an essay.

28 http://www.scanningpens.co.uk/reading-aids/reading-pen-ts-oxford.php

There are also Quicktionary pens that just offer dictionaries and translation of text and the InfoScan TS[29] that will store up to 500 pages of printed text in several different languages. It also allows the user to scan the text directly into any Windows program where it can be edited, read with text to speech, highlighted etc.

It is important to hold the pens at a fairly upright angle, to have clear text and to remember to position them carefully at the beginning of a word so initial letters are not missed. The ear buds help as then you do not have to take the pen to your ear to listen to the voice that is not always that clear. The pens are good at telling you when there are hyphens and you need to scan a new line and the pen screens are fairly easy to read.

Strategies for reading text on the web.

Some technologies will enable any text on screen to be heard. This may be a better solution for older dyslexic students, who wish to read a wider range of articles, for example from the World Wide Web or access texts that are from a scanner or word processor. These tools can be loaded as an extra toolbar and many offer a wide range of features such as highlighting, different voices, dictionaries and note taking support to help with the reading of text and pdf files. The most well know programs that work with browsers and most accessible web pages include ClaroRead[30], TextHelp Read and Write and Dolphin SaySo[31]

---

29 http://www.scanningpens.co.uk/line-scanners/infoscan-ts.php
30 http://www.clarosoftware.com/
31 http://www.yourdolphin.com/

There are also many free versions of text to speech programs that do not offer all the advantages of the programs already mentioned but can offer the reading aloud such as Ivona Mini-Reader[32] or Natural Reader[33] or Balabolka[34]

But it may not just be text to speech that can help when reading web pages. The glare of text on a white background can be uncomfortable and not help with visual stress where text becomes distorted or appears to jump. To help relieve this problem with paper based print coloured overlays are often used. The colour used is a personal choice to suit the individual reader but it is possible to do the same on the screen. A "virtual overlay" is a colour screen option offered by TextHelp Read and Write Gold and ClaroRead. If just a section of the screen needs to be dulled or even highlighted then screen rulers can provide a band of colour over a chosen area on the screen and are available once again from ClaroSoftware, Crossbow[35] or there is the T-Bar as a free download from FX Software[36]

There are also toolbars that can be added to any browser to include text to speech and ways to enlarge the fonts on accessible webpages as well as offering plug-ins that include dictionaries, quick access to important web pages and many other study support mechanisms to help with reading such as clearing the clutter from a page. These plug-ins are all offered on the ATbar [37] which works in any browser and there is an ATbar market place where you can make your own toolbar.

---

32 http://www.ivona.com/en/mini-reader/
33 http://www.naturalreaders.com/
34 http://www.cross-plus-a.com/balabolka.htm
35 http://www.crossboweducation.com/
36 http://www.fxc.btinternet.co.uk/assistive.htm
37 http://www.atbar.org

Each browser has its own plug-ins as well, so you can search the Mozilla Firefox add-ons[38] or the Internet Explorer options[39], the Google Chrome extensions[40] and those for Opera[41] if you always use just one browser. Each has an array of add-ons that change all the time in the way that the mobile phone and tablet app stores are always updating!

Finally and perhaps the easiest option in some cases are the changing of screen settings via the control panel of any personal computer such as colour background and larger menu icons with increased text size and even larger mouse pointers. Some settings can also be changed via the browser that makes accessible web pages easier to read - the BBC offer web pages called My Web My Way[42] to show you how to reach and change your browser settings. It should be noted that some school, college or business networks, where computers are being used by many users, it is not always possible to reach the desktop or browser settings.

In conclusion.

Having successfully worked out the best strategies for reading information online, remembering can be quite another problem – learning how to bookmark or file away 'stuff' is equally important and teaching the art of file naming and categorising information should be an essential part of working online. It is best to develop a good filing system early on with folders that can be coloured or have images to

---

38 https://addons.mozilla.org/
39 http://www.ieaddons.com/gb/
40 https://chrome.google.com/extensions
41 https://addons.opera.com/addons/extensions/
42 http://www.bbc.co.uk/accessibility/

help the memory and programs such as Microsoft OneNote[43] or Evernote[44] that can share saved pictures and documents with links to the original web pages. Mind mapping tools can also be used in this way. There are also many online services that offer storage for the various types of data but all have free storage limits – Dropbox[45], Google Drive[46], Apple iCloud[47] and Microsoft SkyDrive[48].

43 http://office.microsoft.com/en-gb/onenote/
44 http://evernote.com/
45 http://www.dropbox.com/
46 http://www.drive.google.com/
47 http://www.apple.com/icloud/
48 http://windows.microsoft.com/en-US/skydrive/home

Chapter 8 – Free Resources.

Free resources that can support those who need help with their reading and writing difficulties are not so hard to find as they used to be. There are small programs that can be downloaded, used directly on a computer or from a USB pen drive and there are supporting toolbars that can be used alongside other applications such as word processors and browsers. What won't be listed in this chapter are the many interactive online applications that are now available – these can range from full blown word processing services that have already been mentioned such as Google Docs to Mind mapping tools and image sharing sites. Jane Hart author of the website called the Centre for Learning and Performance Technologies lists voting teachers' favourites under her annual top 100 Tools[1]. Many of these sites and others have been evaluated for their accessibility and are stored by activity type on the Web2Access website[2]

Some free assistive technology programs lack the sophistication of the majority of the more commercially developed programs, but they can make up a very useful toolkit. They may not always be updated as regularly as products backed by larger companies so it is important to check the system requirements. Some developers offer a basic version of their program free and ask for support for versions with more features.

The following groups of software tend to be Windows-based but there are also many free Android and Apple programs. It's

---

1   http://c4lpt.co.uk/top-100-tools-for-learning-2011/
2   http://www.web2access.org.uk/activity

important to be aware that some download webpages may not be altogether as secure as one would wish. Always make sure your virus checker is up to date and you have a firewall in place as you need to take care when downloading what are known as executable files (**.exe**). Final health warning! Make sure you have backed up your system, set up a restore point and read the instructions.

Portable USB Pen drive (flash drive) software.

Many small programs can run directly from a pen drive. These usually work on a Microsoft Windows operating system and are known as Portable Apps.[3] The website for these apps has a huge list that can be searched or browsed under various categories including Accessibility with the following offerings:

- Dicom Portable - word completion utility.

- Firefox Accessibility Extension - Make Firefox more accessible.

- On-Screen Keyboard Portable - Easily access an on-screen keyboard.

- Virtual Magnifying Glass Portable - A full-featured screen magnifier.

But there are many more dyslexia friendly apps that can help with access to the web and working online. Craig Mill has put together the Eduapps[4] website which has a selection of apps and ways of working that cover a "range of user requirements to support teaching and learning". The list encompasses:

---

3 http://portableapps.com/
4 http://eduapps.org/

- **AccessApps** – a range of solutions to support writing, reading and planning, as well as sensory, cognitive and physical difficulties.

- **TeachApps** – a collection of software specifically designed for teachers or lecturers.

- **LearnApps** – specifically designed for learners.

- **MyStudyBar** – providing a suite of apps to support literacy that works well when used alongside a word processor.

- **MyVisBar** – a high contrast floating toolbar, designed to support learners with visual difficulties.

- **MyAccess** – accessible applications providing inclusive e-learning options for all.

- **Create&Convert** – support to publish accessible documents and online information for all.

- **Accessible Formatting WordBar** – create accessible Word documents.

Downloadable software.

Many of the technologies available for the pen drives can also be downloaded and used as part of a useful toolkit on any Windows computer. They are often useful on older computers that do not have the power or file space of the later models.

The software has been categorised under the various chapter headings and all can be found under the 'Products' heading > freeware on the EmpTech website[5]

---

5   http://www.emptech.info

Planning, Organisation and Time Management.

Online calendars or ones that synchronise with Google calendar can be very helpful as they can be shared with others. Microsoft Outlook that comes with Microsoft Office offers this support but if you just want a fun desktop saver with reminders try MyCorkboard[6]. There are all sorts of themes and it can be customised to suit your needs with notes and a clock etc.

If you find that you always run out of time it may be worth using TimeLeft[7] that allows you to set times and have reminders with sticky notes plus a stopwatch all on the desktop or there is Stickies[8] from Zhorn Software is a sticky note program for reminders with customisable settings and system tray keystroke access.

Not everyone enjoys making mind maps for planning or organising materials so the other option is myTasks[9], a simple to use 'to do' list with easy categorisation, filters and text based searches and Jot Notes from Kingstairs[10] (these are free 30 day trial programs).

EverNote[11] which is offered as a free download or a service online and even as an app on most phones is not just an instant note maker. You can drag and drop note items from the web, electronic documents and attach pictures to provide a scrolling record of notes, search and work with an entire collection of other programs that allow you to annotate

6   http://www.mycorkboard.com/
7   http://www.timeleft.info/
8   http://www.zhornsoftware.co.uk/stickies/
9   http://kingstairs.com/products/mytasks/
10 http://kingstairs.com/products/jot/
11 http://evernote.com/

videos or turn notes into audio files and make quizzes for revision with Evernote Peek. The company also have a schools section with guides and resources.

However, if mind mapping suits your needs and you can cope with simple style maps then XMind[12] offers you the chance to develop ideas within symbols with icons or on a branch, different layouts and the ability to import and export to other programs including commercial mind mapping applications. There is also Freemind[13] that works with words once again placed on branches rather than in symbols, although it is possible to group items with images and link different concepts.

If you need to organise your files and share them with others then DropBox[14] can be downloaded onto your computer or downloaded onto your mobile as an app and folders can be set up to be shared with whoever you want. It can also be used online in the same way as the Apple iCloud, Microsoft Sky Drive or Google Drive.

Writing.

Whilst writing documents in Microsoft Word it is possible to check the thesaurus and other reference books via the short cut keys 'Shift plus F7', spell checking, autocorrect and autotext can all help. However, if you are not using Microsoft Office it may be worth downloading OpenOffice[15], a free Office suite that supports Microsoft Office files and offers word-processing, spreadsheet, database and drawing

---

12 http://www.xmind.net/
13 http://freemind.sourceforge.net/wiki/index.php/Main_Page
14 http://www.dropbox.com
15 http://www.openoffice.org/

applications. A thesaurus and dictionary that works as a standalone program is WordWeb 6[16] for Windows and as an iPhone app – it offers audio pronunciations, synonyms, confusables and the option of the Oxford and Chambers dictionaries.

When it comes to spell checking this also tends to occur within the word processor which is not always helpful if you are using a simple text editor. This is when FreeSpell and ProSpell[17] can be helpful or tinySpell 1.9[18] which checks spelling in Windows applications and web forms where there is no built in spell checker. It is worth downloading the British English Dictionary when you download this spell checker which can also be used on a pendrive.

Typing practice is also available for free and there are the options of Analytical Eye Typing Tutor[19] which was originally developed for schools with text based files that can be adapted to suit user needs or Senselang Touch Typing[20] which has a large collection of lessons, games and tests.

If speed is still an issue or word finding is difficult then it is possible that word prediction may help – **A.I.Type**[21] is available for the PC, Android phone and can be found on ATbar. It offers users a selection of words as you type. Another option is eType[22] that offers auto-completion with a dictionary or translation if you want to use other languages.

16 http://wordweb.info/
17 http://hcidesign.com/freespell/
18 http://tinyspell.numerit.com/
19 http://www.aetech.co.uk/ttutor/
20 http://www.sense-lang.org/typing/
21 http://www.aitype.com/index.php/download
22 http://www.etype.com/

Both programs work in any text editing situation whether on or off line.

Finally if you want a really simple word processor that will work well for younger writers try Edword[23] as it has a reduced number of menu items but looks very similar to Microsoft Word and has all the basics needed. It can be used with text to speech programs and symbols[24]

Reading.

There are now many free apps for reading ebooks on mobile phones and tablets but often these ebook readers are also available for download examples include Kindle, Blio, Stanza and Kobo. If you want to use Daisy books that guarantee text to speech then AMIS[25] that has been designed for those with visual impairments will read Daisy Talking Books as well the free TPB Reader[26]. Neither have a particularly special interface but they can be useful if fonts and colours also need to be changed to aid reading.

WordTalk[27] provides text to speech feedback and text highlighting when proofreading in Microsoft Word. There are plenty of other text to speech readers such NaturalReader[28] that works with Internet Explorer, Word, Adobe Reader, Outlook and plain text. ReadPlease 2003[29] reads anything on the screen that you can highlight with the mouse or copy

---

23 http://www.softpedia.com/get/Internet/Browsers/EdWord.shtml
24 http://www.softpedia.com/get/Internet/Browsers/EdWord.shtml
25 http://www.daisy.org/amis/
26 http://www.tpb.se/english/talking_books/reading_programmes_and_players/
27 http://www.wordtalk.org.uk/
28 http://www.naturalreaders.com/
29 http://www.readplease.com/

to the clip board and sits in the system tray ready for use or works directly with Microsoft Word and Internet Explorer.

If reading on screen causes visual stress it may be worth trying the options offered by FX Software[30] such as the T-Bar that covers an area of the screen with a tinted overlay and the Vu-bar on-screen ruler that can be used to follow text on any application.

Finally in this section if you are worried about the reading level of a book or some text or even a web page then Reading Level Calculator is a tool that can estimate the level based on word length and syllables.

Numeracy.

Some calculators that come as part of the computer or tablets operating system are small and not very student friendly. It may be worth trying the Big Simple Talking Calculator[31] which is a full screen calculator that is easy to read with speech output for answers. Power Calculator 1.5[32] allows for many more complex mathematical functions and the FRS Talking Calculator[33] is an onscreen talking calculator with large keys and the sums are seen vertically – ideal for younger users.

Working on the web.

This last section will not be looking at apps for portable technologies but the add-ons or plug-ins that can be used with browsers such as text to speech and dictionaries etc.

30 http://www.fxc.btinternet.co.uk/assistive.htm
31 http://www.softpedia.com/get/Science-CAD/Big-Simple-Talking-Calculator.shtml
32 http://www.softpedia.com/get/Others/Home-Education/Power-Calculator-Chen.shtml
33 http://fastrabbitsoftware.com/talking_calculator.htm

British Dyslexia Association Membership.

The British Dyslexia Association offers a wide range of membership options. This includes individual, organisational and local dyslexia associations.

By becoming a member of the B.D.A. you will be entitled to a host of benefits, including:

- Dyslexia Contact magazine.

- E-newsletter 3 times per year.

- Discount on B.D.A. conferences.

- Discount on B.D.A. open training events.

- Consultation on key policy issues.

- Discounted price the Dyslexia Journal.

- Option to receive a Dyslexia Handbook each year.

Full details of the various types of membership and how to join can be found on our website, **www.bdadyslexia.org.uk/membership.html**. Alternatively, you can contact the Membership team on 0845-251-9003.

There are addon or plug-in market places for all the main web browsers These have been mentioned and they are worth visiting although they are about as daunting as the app stores.

If it just text to speech that is required when surfing the net it is worth trying programs that work across all browsers such as BrowseAloud[34] that works with pages that have subscribed to this TextHelp application and it offers hover highlighting, text selection, translator and dictionary, screen masking and an MP3 Maker. The readers mentioned above such as ReadPlease 2003 and NaturalReader will also read accessible web pages.

ATbar[35] is a toolbar that can be added as a 'bookmark' or 'favorite' to all the main browsers and it will provide text to speech, spell checking, a dictionary, the chance to change the look and feel of the web pages if possible, as well as word prediction to help with text creation. Many other plugins can be added via the market place such as Readable that clears the clutter from pages or various calculators and thesauri and translators.

But going back to the individual browsers that have their own plugins here are just a few that have been tried and tested.

The Mozilla Firefox Toolbar Additions[36] include a plugin to change the background colour of a website with **Color That Site**! or just the tabs on your browser with **Colorfultabs**. **Wikilook** and **Dictionary.com** provide information and

---

34 http://www.browsealoud.com/page.asp?pg_id=80002&tile=UK
35 http://www.atbar.org
36 https://addons.mozilla.org/en-US/firefox/

definitions and **Text to Voice 1.05** allows for sections of accessible web pages to be read aloud.

The toolbar additions for Internet Explorer[37] include **CleanPage** that reduce web page clutter, the **ieSpell** for instant spell checking in forms that do not have a built in spell checker. **RoboForm password manager** is very helpful if you tend to forget your passwords and **VozMe** [38]provides text to speech.

Google's Chrome browser uses its own toolbar to provide spell checking, translation along with extensions[39] such as **Voice Search Chrome** for dictating in queries and **After the Deadline** spell checker. Its version of password support is called **LastPass** password manager and there is the hand **Webscreen shot** for taking snapshots of more than the screen size, **Easy Reader** will clear clutter from the webpages and **MyNotesApp** is there for instant notes whilst surfing.

You do not always have to be online to run Chrome apps in your browser. Google have a list of apps that may be useful when you are offline[40] such as Gmail, Google calendar, Quick note, Jolicloud, Scientific calculator, Task Timer, and World clock (You do not need to Google the time of various countries or depend on your desktop clock settings).

Although not such a popular browser, Opera[41] has some very useful mouse gestures for flicking between pages and also offers voice dictation and **Autocomplete for the text input**

---

37 http://www.iegallery.com/Addonsthose
38 http://vozme.com/bookmarklet.php?lang=en
39 https://chrome.google.com/webstore/category/extensions?hl=en
40 https://chrome.google.com/webstore/category/collection/offline_enabled?utm_source=chrome-ntp-icon
41 https://addons.opera.com/en/extensions/

box. It has password support with **Password hasher**, a handy scientific **Calculator** and **Taskboard** for jobs that need to be done.

Safari [42]can be used on all computers not just the Apple Mac and it has an app for creating passwords, **1Password** can create passwords and easy PDF reader called **PDF Browser Plugin** and **Cooliris** for full screen picture and video watching.

All of these add-ons or extensions and toolbars are just the tip of the iceberg when it comes to finding free programs for your computer and portable technologies. The internet is full of blogs and wikis written by experts and 'not so experts' telling you about the latest app or piece of software that might help – it really is a case of buyer beware and asking those who have already tried some free options as opposed to the commercial assistive technologies. Freeware can provide an easy way to try ideas that might help with studying or work but many are not specifically designed to support dyslexia. There is always the B.D.A. helpline and the website run by the B.D.A. New Technologies committee[43] – do make contact if you are worried about any choices concerning the use of assistive technologies.

---

42 **http://extensions.apple.com/**
43 **http://bdatech.org/**

Chapter 9 – Case Studies.

Choosing, Evaluating and Using Assistive Technology.
By Neil Cottrell.

Assistive technology is software or hardware (or a combination of both) that is designed to help you overcome barriers that would otherwise prevent you from working effectively. It usually runs alongside the software packages you already use, providing new features or modifying how you use your computer. Unlike learning software, which teaches you a specific skill until you have mastered it, assistive technology is intended for long-term and everyday use.

In this chapter I will discuss some of the techniques and processes that you should use when deciding what assistive technology is best for you or the dyslexic person you are supporting. The chapter is split into three sections: **Choosing**, **Evaluating** and **Using** Assistive Technology. I'll also talk about my own experiences with dyslexia and how I used assistive technology to overcome my difficulties.

Before I dive into the details, there are three key things that you should remember:

Everyone's different: dyslexia affects people in different ways. So what works for someone you know may not necessarily be suitable for you. It's therefore important to learn about and try as much assistive technology as possible before you make your final decisions.

Focus on Coping Strategies: when deciding upon what assistive technology to use, think first about your own difficulties, and then use assistive technology as a coping strategy to overcome those difficulties.

Time investment: By taking the time to carefully choose, evaluate and use assistive software you will get the maximum benefit. In the long run, you will save time and money, and avoid frustration.

Keeping these three principles in mind will help you to make the right choices, by developing coping strategies that are tailored to your specific needs.

A final thing to keep in mind throughout this chapter is that assistive technology is not always the best solution; it may be that the software you already use, or software that is free to download, can be an effective coping strategy. Examples of this include task management software, calendar apps or your operating system's built in display or accessibility settings. Some coping strategies may not involve technology at all, such as using a coloured 'reading ruler' to reduce the stark contrast on a page of text. So don't be afraid to think outside the box in order to develop coping strategies that work for you.

My Story.

I am severely dyslexic. I was diagnosed at the age of 10 and had a statement of special educational need by age 12. I relied completely on assistive technology throughout secondary school, and benefited from brilliant support from my parents and teachers. All in all, I consider myself very lucky; without this support as well as extra tuition to help with my difficulties and a laptop provided by my Local Education Authority, I would have failed many of my GCSEs and left school at 16.

Alongside this support, I developed and adapted coping strategies that helped to put me on a level-playing field with my peers. By properly identifying my issues and crafting coping strategies to address them I've made my dreams a reality, graduating from university with first class honours and starting and growing a successful company.

Choosing Assistive Technology.

Choosing assistive technology is the first and arguably the most important step in the process, as the initial choices you make will greatly influence the success of your coping strategies. Make sure to look at as many products as possible. Choosing software that is used by people you know has obvious benefits – it will be easy to get help and advice from people you trust – but keep in mind that there may be ideal solutions that they have never come across. Another good resource is suppliers (companies who sell a wide range of assistive technology), who should be able to match your needs to the features and benefits of different solutions.

Assistive Technology as Coping Strategies.

A coping strategy is the best way to compensate for your difficulties. It's very important to work on improving your existing skills, but coping strategies are just as vital because they help you to develop what I call high-level skills. It's essential that these high-level skills, such as analytical thinking and forming opinions, are allowed to develop regardless of any difficulties with lower-level skills such as reading, spelling or memory. So the aim of a coping strategy is to get around low-level difficulties, to allow you to develop your high-level skills.

The diagram opposite demonstrates how the task of analysing a poem can be made easier by using assistive technology.

By looking at your difficulties from the lowest possible level, you can develop coping strategies that suit your specific needs, and choose assistive technology to match. For example, if you have problems with reading, find out what it is that makes reading so difficult. Are you unable to focus on the words on your screen? If so, maybe screen-tinting – where a soft colour such as pale yellow is applied over your screen – is all you need. Or is it that you can see the letters fine, but you're unable to decode them into words or sentences that you can understand? If that's the case, text-to-speech software, where text is spoken by a synthesised voice is probably your best bet. Likewise, there are multiple approaches to improving your organisation, from detailed day planners through to mind-mapping software. Whatever your difficulties, make sure you fully understand the underlying issues before deciding what tools you need.

How to decide what's best for you.

Once you've established exactly what your difficulties are and the best way to overcome them, it's time to really look at what's available. Before doing your own research, seek advice and guidance from the experts. A great place to start

Analysing a Poem

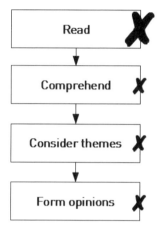

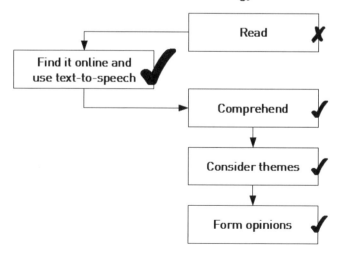

is the B.D.A.'s own Technology website, **BDATech.org**, which gives recommendations on a wide range of software. Other good resources include **Lexdis.org.uk** and **EmpTech.info**. Offline you can speak to teachers, learning support assistants, disability specialists and other users of assistive technology to find out what they recommend and why. Overall, it's important to take a really good look; invest plenty of time looking at all the options. For each solution you should consider not only features and unique selling points but also benefits, ease of use and of course price. Finally, throughout the process remember to relate your research back to the specific issues that you have.

Evaluating Assistive Technology.

At this point you should have sought out advice and recommendations for a wide range of products. As I've said, the amount of time you invest when choosing assistive technology is very important, and this is no less important during the evaluation stage. Try lots of different pieces of technology by downloading free trials, making sure to look at individual settings and different ways that the software can be used. You can also learn more about the software by viewing video tutorials. Just like at the choosing stage, you should speak to users of assistive software, teachers and disability specialists to find out what they like and don't like about each package. And if the solution isn't working as you'd hoped then ask the developers – assistive technology companies are usually very happy to give support and guidance, and also to hear your ideas about their products.

Take your time.

When evaluating assistive technology, you should really make the most of free trials; use software throughout the trial period (often 30 days) instead of just trying it once. When you're relaxed and have time to spare then you can try out every feature in multiple combinations. But you should also try using the same program when you're stressed and need to get things done. Does it work in practice, or just in theory?

Take text-to-speech software as an example: using synchronised highlighting to show what's being read might be useful when you have the time to go through things thoroughly, but sometimes when I'm stressed I find it easier to just get the gist of the text by closing my eyes and letting the words wash over me. As you develop coping strategies using individual pieces of software, see if these strategies hold up when you're stressed. If not, try changing some settings or finding a different way to use that product. If it doesn't work when you really need it then you'll have saved yourself some money!

Alternatives.

For every difficulty that you have, there will be multiple products that attempt to provide a coping strategy, but it's worth spending the time to consider how they're different. For example, there is a good choice of products that allow you to scan books, turning them into documents that can be spoken aloud. Yet each one will do certain things better and other things slightly worse. It's often a matter of personal preference and opinions will vary, so try similar products to find one that meets your needs.

Another approach is to look at products that tackle the same issue but in different ways. For people who have issues with spelling, dictation can be an excellent solution: instead of typing you can simply speak. On the other hand, if you don't have issues with typing and don't want to change the way you work, then using autocorrection software might suit you better. Remember: everyone's different, so consider software that makes use of alternative coping strategies as part of your research.

Combinations.

Before you make your final decisions it's also important to test different products in combination with each other. After all, in order to get the most benefit you'll need to develop multiple coping strategies, often with individual products for each one. If two packages will help you, and you can afford it, go for both of them! So when you've narrowed down your choices, make sure that they work together without any problems; don't just rely on others saying that they are compatible.

Using Assistive Technology.

If you've followed my advice so far, then you'll have done your research properly and have created coping strategies that meet your own specific needs. This is where you will really start to benefit. The importance of time investment continues into this stage, because by doing so you'll greatly reduce the potential for annoyance and frustration. Keep in mind, though, that the amount of time that you'll need to invest will vary from product to product.

When you get the opportunity, go deeply into every feature and menu, trying the software in lots of different scenarios. You might discover new features or alternative approaches to using the software, or find situations where you can and can't use it. This will help you to establish where the boundaries are and where it can help you most. At this stage, why not go back and have a look at the video tutorials again?

Making the most of assistive technology.

If the software's right for you then it will often start to make your life easier from the moment you install it. For example, pressing play for text to be spoken aloud is easy to do and you will get used to it quickly. But you can get even more benefit by customising the software: by tweaking the settings, defining shortcut keys or turning off features that you don't need. As I've said throughout this chapter, everyone's different, so use your software in the way that's best for you.

Conclusion.

There are three key things that I want you to take away from this chapter. Firstly, **everyone's different**, so choose the technology that's best for you. Secondly, you should always **develop coping strategies that meet your specific needs**, and then pick assistive technology to fit. Thirdly, **investing time**, particularly at the start, will be really worth your while. It's also important to keep re-evaluating how you're using assistive software, making tweaks as necessary. Finally, you should keep an eye out for new products: the assistive technology industry is constantly producing innovative new solutions, and your perfect coping strategy might be just around the corner. Assistive technology can make such an amazing difference when you've got it right, enabling you to overcome your difficulties and really reach your full potential.

You can find out more about Neil's own coping strategies and the assistive technology he uses here:
www.LexAble.com/Neil_Coping_Strategies

Assistive Technology for Independent Learning (ATIL) Project at Stanbridge Earls School.
By Robert Bailey.

School Description.

Stanbridge Earls is a specialist coeducational boarding and day school. The majority of students on roll have recognised SpLDs, including dyslexia, dyspraxia and dyscalculia.

- The school currently has four consecutive outstanding reports from Ofsted and the Independent Schools Inspectorate (ISI) and holds specialist provision status with the Council for the Registration of Schools Teaching Dyslexic Pupils (CReSTeD).

- Stanbridge Earls is not a school that solely focuses on examination grades. The school's ethos is to rebuild confidence in its young people by taking a holistic approach to education. Children that have struggled in their previous schools often arrive low in self-confidence and need boosting before they are prepared to take on new learning challenges. A breadth of experiences is delivered with participation and effort celebrated on a par with performance levels. As confidence grows so attitudes to learning are re-built.

School Review.

During the summer term of 2009 the school undertook a trial of Assistive Technology (AT) wares, including speech recognition software, audio note takers and digital recorders. It proved to be a successful trial and showed a spectrum of potential gains for students, staff and the school as a whole.

Specific students moved from producing single paragraphs of limited text to consistently producing multiple pages of quality work, independently during evening preps.

In March 2010, ISI reported the quality of academic and other achievements, pupils' personal development and the effectiveness of governance, leadership and management to be excellent or outstanding. The school was advised to:

Further investigate and develop the use of existing expertise amongst staff to provide training, in particular in working with pupils with SEN and the use of ICT for all staff.

Continue to research and stay abreast of the latest developments in technology to support pupils with SEN.

Identified Priorities.

As a direct result of stakeholder consultations and strategic planning the school focussed its key academic aim on developing outstanding teaching and learning by making the best use of technological developments. The senior management team directed the introduction of specialist BDA training for its entire mainstream academic staff. The school introduced a two-year trial of improved learning resources using AT for its sixth form students.

ATIL Project Details

Proposed advancements included:

1. Development of a dedicated study room within a new sixth form centre.

2. Provision of individual lap top computers for all sixth form students.

3. Provision of personalised software and additional AT, such as audio recorders; to best meet the individual needs of students and facilitate the development of skills for independent learning.

4. Employment of additional specialist technology staff, to support training, prep organisation and production in this learning environment.

5. Provision of training on use hardware and software to both students and staff.

Key objective was to enable students the freedom to work using their own skills and strengths.

Specialist guidance was sought from a world-renowned visiting Educational Psychologist, Dr Alexakis Lannigan, regarding ways to improve its educational provision. Further research was undertaken to discover cutting edge AT for SpLD students. Several leading international universities indicated the types of independent learning skills that they expect of their undergraduates and detailed friendly software. Initial guidance and subsequent research informed the compilation of software contents for a student toolbox.

A software toolbox was provided to each student via their laptop including the following:

1. **Audio Notetaker** software, which helped students with navigating, annotating and organising digital recordings delivering a visual representation of what was being listened to.

2. **Browse-aloud** software, which provided a text to speech facility, which also read websites making it a useful research tool.

3. **Dragon Naturally Speaking 10** voice recognition software was made available on a selective basis via specialist staff within the school's Accelerated Learning Centre (ALC). Provision followed individual assessment on suitability supported by individual teaching.

4. **DS-65 digital recorders** were used to record dictations, discussions or personal notes and could then be reviewed using Dragon software.

5. **Ecopy** enabled students to create and distribute PDF files through document scanning without complex software applications. Optical Character Recognition (OCR) allowed students to convert scanned documents into editable text documents that could then be used in TextHelp.

6. **Inspiration**, a mind-mapping programme, helped develop visual thinking and learning, helping students to think, brainstorm, organise, analyse and write. This proved useful for SpLD students with difficulties organising ideas and planning written work. It was also helpful for planning and structuring essays, creating revision notes and writing up lesson notes.

7. **TextHelp Read & Write Gold** was used by students, to hear their own work read back.

8. **Thinkmap Visual Thesaurus** delivered an online visual thesaurus and dictionary.

9. **Verity-Spell** software provided a dyslexia friendly spelling and grammar checker.

10. **Wordbar**, an on-line writing tool, sat alongside the word processor, providing almost instant access to words and phrases for chosen topics.

The project was launched with an Open Day at the school, with technology exhibitions and technology exhibitor presentations. BBC television attended the launch, filmed students using ATIL resources and produced a segment for their South Today evening news.

Training was introduced for students to raise their basic IT and more specific software skills.

In-service training was also delivered to academic staff in a bid to maximise progress, to improve delivery of information within lessons, using AT.

Individual assessment at Stanbridge Earls now occurs in reading and spelling twice per year. The Gray Silent Reading Test and the Wide Range Ability Test (WRAT4) for spelling have been adopted as the school's preferred tests. The school's Special Educational Needs Co-ordinator (SENCo) has developed the central SEN register to identify each pupil's assessment scores, recognised needs and subsequent provision. Each student's reading and spelling results are standardised for norm reference and age equivalence is calculated to indicate the degree of skill delay.

Professional review was developed to include an additional lesson observation descriptor within the academic performance management system, relating to information delivery through the use of AT.

What next?

The school has established a working partnership with Kellogg College at the University of Oxford. In turn, the college has established the Centre for Research into Assistive Learning Technologies. Lorna McKnight, a Kellogg College researcher, has been appointed to monitor the ATIL project, to conduct an extensive review of academic literature with a view to feeding into the future phases of the project and reporting findings that will support the wider uptake of appropriate forms of technology support for SpLD students.

Kellogg's mantra is lifelong learning, which fits nicely with the school's aim to develop independent learning skills that students take beyond the school gates.

The early findings of Oxford research are positive, showing gains for senior students. The software that the students are using seem to have benefits for their working practice, with all students identifying at least one piece of software as having helped them in their work. The software seems to offer a benefit to independent work, and for a number has provided a level of independence that would otherwise not be possible.

The project was highly ambitious in terms of the work proposed within its initial timescale, and therefore these positive outcomes, although on a reasonably small scale at present, represent a respectable level of achievement to date.

It has been recognised that introducing assistive technology at age 16 years is too late as learning habits are already developed and become difficult to adapt.

As a result the school aims to expand AT learning provision and resources, beginning in September 2012. Discrete lessons in AT will be delivered to all students in Key Stage 3 (Years 7, 8 and 9).

The school's primary internal objective is to develop a coordinated approach to the delivery of AT across the whole school.

Secondary external objectives include the school's aim to become recognised as a centre of excellence for using AT to level the playing field or rather 'learning field' for SpLD students. Further, it is hoped that project outcomes, in liaison with Oxford University research, will influence practice across the education sector including examination boards. As AT becomes a part of each student's normal working practice, it seems logical that this approach should be recognised by the examination boards within the scope for improved access arrangements.

For further information on the ATIL project developments, please contact Dean Williams, project chair from September 2012, at: **dean.williams@stanbridgeearls.co.uk**

Introduction of Speech Recognition Software to assist a 10-year-old boy.
By Malcolm Litten.

AZ was referred for a full assessment while in Year 5 because of his severe problems with the production of written work. His reading was not a problem in the same way.

As a result of the assessment, the recommendation was made that he should try using speech recognition software. His assessor explains her thinking about this recommendation in the following way:

"Where an individual's handwriting is awful or even illegible and they find spelling very difficult and they may say something like, 'I find it difficult to get what's in my brain on to paper,' speech recognition may well provide an answer. What I recognise is a discrepancy between the individual's verbal skills and their 'recording' work – what they can write or type. Although typing skills may overcome some of the problems, if spelling remains a big problem it can obstruct the train of thought the individual is attempting to record. Unfortunately, in education, the requirement to write may mean the teacher cannot know what is going on in a student's brain if they cannot see it on paper."

As a result of the recommendation, AZ received training in the use of speech recognition software, specifically *Dragon NaturallySpeaking*. The training consisted of four hour-long sessions spread out over a fortnight. This training involved enabling the software to recognise his voice by reading a prescribed passage to the computer. This resulted in his speech being successfully recognised by the software – somewhere near the 95% accuracy claimed by the manufacturers. The second and third training sessions focused on the best manner of delivery when dictating and the routines to follow when correcting any errors in recognition. The final session addressed methods of preparation when undertaking longer pieces of writing. Throughout training, the software was only used under the trainer's supervision in order to establish the best habits in the trainee. After training, the trainee was encouraged to undertake ten sessions of 10-15 minutes dictation and correction to ensure these habits were firmly established.

AZ has only used speech recognition at home, not in school. His teachers have supported this practice by encouraging him to prepare a plan for longer written pieces in class and then create them for homework.

His mother describes the difference between AZ undertaking such work before and after the introduction of speech recognition: "Before, getting him to do the work was always a struggle – it was like pulling teeth. Since, he is keen to do it because he knows he can. He actually loved doing a project on the Armada. He insisted on doing more each evening for a week. There was no stopping him!"

AZ himself recognises a huge difference. He used to become very anxious whenever written work was required, mentioning "sweaty palms." Spelling was a major problem. Now *Dragon* takes care of that. He knows he now gets more words down. But interestingly, he has also become less anxious about doing bits of handwriting in school.

AZ has now been using *Dragon* for over a year. Both he and his mother say his confidence has grown in a much more general way. At the end of Year 6 he was awarded a Merit at school for his improved commitment and hard work and his progress particularly in English and history – the two subjects that consistently require longer pieces of writing from him.

His history teacher is equally clear about the differences she sees. His work has greatly improved so that now he is among the best in the class. She sees the same improvement in his general confidence. She has begun recommending *Dragon* to other parents. (AZ is convinced one of his friends should be using it!)

He is not using *Dragon* daily. He estimated he might have a task for which he used it every three weeks. He has used it for other purposes like writing thank you letters. He finds no difficulty in remembering how to use the software despite these gaps. He reports no disadvantages in working in this way.

His mother is delighted by what has happened. "He's had it all in his head and now he can demonstrate it. It's been a fantastic improvement."

Chapter 10 – What next...?

Sir Tim Berners-Lee, (inventor of the World Wide Web) in a presentation to the United States House of Representatives in March 2007 said:

> *"So how do we plan for a better future, better for society?*
>
> *We ensure that that both technological protocols and social conventions respect basic values. That the Web remains a universal platform: independent of any specific hardware device, software platform, language, culture, or disability."*[1]

So we know we want software and hardware to all work together and for it to be accessible to all in the widest sense. But we at present that dream for the future has yet to materialise, although technology is becoming increasingly more available to a wider group of people. No one can escape the rapid rise in the use of portable devices that can be connected to the internet, enhancing and in some cases even replacing the traditional computers we have used in the past. Young children can be seen using tablet technologies in their primary schools and it is rare that a young person will willingly lose their mobile phone.

Most young people are automatically using the built in assistive technologies on a mobile such as predictive text typing but not being aware that this might help on their school computers. On some phones it is so easy to take a photograph, video clip or sound recording and email it to friends or send it to what is now known as a social network on the web to share with many others. This use of

1   http://dig.csail.mit.edu/2007/03/01-ushouse-future-of-the-web.html

multimedia, that can be so helpful to those with dyslexia, requires separate equipment such as a camera, scanner and greater skill on a traditional computer and somehow loses the ingredient of fun when it has to set up as a lesson.

The creative use of technologies needs to be explored at all stages in the young person's educational journey to encourage different ways of learning and successful outcomes for all. As Thomas West (who wrote 'In the Mind's Eye') said in an interview in 2005:

> *"I believe the powerful changes in computer-visualization technology will change our culture as much as the printing press did in the past. New visualization technologies will show us a side of our brains that has mostly atrophied.*
>
> *This isn't frivolous, like entertainment television, which you watch passively. This technology is interactive and very powerful in delivering lots of information. It will allow us to educate a wider band of individuals and keep people engaged far more than any lecture could. This technology will tap into human brain power in virtually every field."*[2]

Information is presented to us everywhere in multi-media formats with high quality video, animation and sound, from TV advertisements and programmes to clips on YouTube, which can be both entertaining and instructive. Depending upon how these technologies are incorporated and accepted as part of everyday classroom practice, dyslexic difficulties may no longer become the hindrance to school progress

2   http://www.washingtonian.com/articles/health/secrets-of-the-brain-dyslexia-interview-with-thomas-west/

- an experience that has occurred with others in the past. However, it remains to be seen how long it takes for a suitable means of assessment to be developed to replace the existing emphasis upon the hand written examination system and to enable such skills to be suitably recognised.

Major changes in technology that have affected us all and need to be understood and embraced include Apple's chic designs with high resolution displays on **iPads, iPhones and iPods**, the explosion of different **Android devices** with free apps and finally **Windows 8 and gesture based computing**. On the web we have **cloud computing** – a grand name for working with tools over the internet that are often free and easy to use and may be recognised as web services, storage areas and apps. All these innovations allow us to use technology when and where we like as long as we can afford to purchase them and are able to get a connection!

iPads, iPhones and iPods.

At the time of writing the devices that have been causing greatest excitement have been the Apple iPad and its smaller relations the iPod Touch and iPhone. Educational establishments across the world are beginning to realise the enormous potential of these devices. Although other tablet computers with operating systems such as Android and Microsoft Windows 8 exist, it may take some time for these systems to overtake the lead currently offered by Apple's iOS.

In the UK some schools have already made small numbers of iPads available to their pupils, whilst others have issued them to all their students and incorporated their use in their curriculum, with considerable success if recent Ofsted reports are to be taken into account. There are regional Apple Training Centres around the world[3] which provide support and training to schools using their equipment. Around the UK some of these are based in schools such as Bohunt School in Hampshire[4]. Their document on 'Transforming Learning' is particularly interesting[5] and encompasses the latest ideas on effective learning. Another school at Clevedon in North Somerset is gradually developing its iPad use and also has an informative website.[6]

So what is it about these devices that is creating such enthusiasm?

Multimedia making hardware is there in one convenient portable device - camera with video, sound recording and playback, wifi access with the bonus of good battery life and excellent screen resolution.

The range of software, in the form of apps, is vast and rapidly expanding. Most of the commercial products offer cut down versions of their desktop equivalents at a cheaper price compared to their desktop equivalents. For example Pages, which is Apple's flagship document creator, costs £6.99. There are also many free apps, for example Dragon Dictation, which offers speech recognition when connected to the internet, image to text for optical character recognition, dictionaries, thesauri and mind mapping tools.

---

3   http://www.apple.com/uk/education/rtc/
4   www.bohunt.hants.sch.uk/AppleRTC.aspx
5   www.bohunt.hants.sch.uk/Downloads/Regional%20Training%20Centre/
    TechTransformingLearning_BohuntSch_v4.pdf
6   www.iclevedon.co.uk

Unlike larger software packages for traditional computers, many apps address single functions, which can then be integrated into the user's project. For example, a piece of text created in the Dragon app can be copied and pasted into Pages or wherever it is needed using just a few taps on the screen. Craig Mill has provided a diagrammatic guide to "iPad Apps and integrative workflows to support learners with literacy difficulties/dyslexia" on the CALL Scotland website.[7]

The iPad can be used as a portable interactive whiteboard via a projector or to a large TV screen. This means that lesson notes, extracts from the internet or wherever can be carried around and distributed digitally to the class or shared when working collaboratively.

Challenge Based Learning.

As with any new technology, training is essential for effective use. As in the early days of computers in schools, it is not unusual to find that the pupils themselves are the best teachers. Working together on a project is often the best way to improve individual skills and confidence. This approach, which is called 'Challenge Based Learning', aims to better prepare learners for the world ahead of them

This extract from an American website about Challenged based learning[8] explains more...

"Traditional teaching and learning models are becoming increasingly ineffective with a generation of students who have instant access to vast amounts of information, embrace

---

7   http://www.callscotland.org.uk/Blog/Blog-Post/index.php?reference=331
8   www.challengebasedlearning.org

the roles of content producer and publisher and have access to extensive online social networks.

Today, students are often faced with assignments and assessments that lack a real-world context. Many of these students either learn to do just enough to get by or they lose interest altogether and drop out. In this interconnected world, with ubiquitous access to powerful technologies, new models of teaching and learning are possible, and engagement is paramount to meeting the needs of more students."

The Essex primary school at Flitch Green is an example of this approach to learning and details of their approach is being used as a promotional example by Apple on their education section.[9]

Android devices.

These devices may not have such an ardent following as the Apple iOS devices but there are many more options and the costs are much reduced. The devices themselves are cheaper but may not offer quite the same high resolution screens as the iPad or guarantees for the robustness of the apps developed as they do not go through a standardisation process as required by Apple . There is a good range of sizes from the 7 inch to 10 inch tablets offering similar features to the iPad. The bonus on Android is that you can spend time downloading or changing the themes on the device even tweaking the operating system settings in many more ways than on the iPad. The system integrates closely with all the Google Apps and Google Voice offers speech control.

---

9   **www.apple.com**/education/profiles/flitch-green/#video-flitch-green

Android has several app stores that work in a similar way to the Apple App store offering a description of the app, the systems with which it works and a download link. You do not have to download via one store and there are many options for trialling the more expensive apps.

The Android operating system is often hidden behind other names such as the Barnes and Noble Nook and Amazon Kindle Fire ereaders, which offer cut-down versions of Android rather than a fully-fledged system as is seen in the Samsung Galaxy or the Toshiba tablets The fact that there are hardware options means that the user has some choices when it comes to screen size from around 7 – 10 inches.

At the time of writing there appear to be very few schools publicising their use of Android tablets, but the Android operating system on various mobile phones seems to be more popular when compared to the iPhone according to the mobile tracker on **uswitch.com**[10] perhaps due to the lower cost. There are websites that can help with the use of Android in schools such as Android4Schools[11] written by Richard Byrne an American teacher who also has a blog about free technologies for teachers and Android for Education[12] by David Andrade another American teacher. Finally there are some useful tips and tricks on Android for Academics[13]

---

10 http://www.uswitch.com/mobiles/mobile_tracker/
11 http://www.android4schools.com/
12 http://educationaltechnologyguy.blogspot.co.uk/p/android-for-education.html
13 http://androidforacademics.com/tipstricks/

Windows 8 and Windows RT (for certain tablets).

Windows 8 will be launched in the UK at the end of October 2012, but those who have been following its development will be aware that this operating system has been designed with the tablet and touch screen in mind. It will work across laptops and tablets as well as desktops and allows the user to flip between a highly graphical view to a classic view[14]. It could be very dyslexia friendly when user settings have been adjusted and may be a winning combination for those who wish to stay with Microsoft. One plus point for using a Windows 8 tablet is the ease with which it is possible to move from one user account to another.

Accessing the Windows tablet touch interface is similar to other tablets with swipes and gestures using different movements of the finger tips but there do not appear to be any complex moves involving four or five finger gestures as with the Apple iPad. Built in handwriting recognition is offered as an alternative to typing text and the fact that you will be able to share data between apps more easily than is currently possible on other tablet operating systems may be useful.

Microsoft has a Windows phone apps site[15] that provides users with an insight into the type of apps available but there is very little that can be said about how the apps will work on the next batch of tablets. It hard to imagine how Microsoft can catch up on the 33,000 educational apps available on the Apple apps store[16]

---

14 http://www.dedoimedo.com/computers/windows-8-settings.html
15 http://www.windowsphone.com/en-GB/apps
16 http://www.cultofmac.com/186533/why-window-8-tablets-will-lose-to-the-ipad-in-education-feature/

Pros and cons of tablet technologies:

- Access to facilities in one device e.g as said above camera, voice recorder, text but can be quickly linked together to create presentations e.g. SoundPics.

- Access to ebooks e.g. apps for Blio, Kindle (but not necessarily speech enabled) and audiobooks on one device (but enhance study with use of note taking facilities, definitions etc.

- Portability and freedom from cables.

- Apps that are cheaper than regular computer software packages (but …)

- Easy to purchase apps that can be downloaded immediately from an online market place.

- Onscreen keyboards which negate the need for a mouse

- Collaboration – not just portability but by sharing screens (easy to mirror screens onto a whiteboard or larger screen by using AppleTV or apps such as Reflection.

A few Cons to consider.

- Apps provide byte-sized access to functions which may be sufficient for some whilst others may need greater support offered by laptops and full versions of software.

- On-screen keyboards may not suit or be comfortable for extended periods of writing – consider purchase of a separate keyboard or folio type keyboard.

- Abundance of apps of assorted quality on the market place – need to exert caution and use trial versions before purchasing but this takes time.

- Caution: may not always provide the best solution e.g. not everything on the screen can yet be accessed with a web-reader, text to speech or a 'Speak Selection' facility.

Cloud Computing.

The internet is an exciting place to be for children, young people and adults but before suggesting some useful ways of making the most of 'Cloud Computing', it is important that rules are followed to ensure safe surfing and to avoid computer viruses and spam etc. The Get Safe Online[17] website has much to offer in terms of free and unbiased information on the subject. The BBC also has some useful advice on their Connect Online[18] site with a video.

Having made sure you are aware of the pitfalls related to passwords, uploading private information and downloading suspect files it is time to realise that you can use the internet as a service in the same way that you use your Office programs. Cloud computing offers services that would in the past, have been downloaded onto a computer. This means you can work anywhere, so long as you are connected. You can plan projects, draw pictures and write documents as well as save the files with for instance a range of Google Apps[19]. Anything you have created can be shared by using Dropbox[20], Google Drive[21] and Windows SkyDrive[22] or Apple iCloud[23]

17   https://www.getsafeonline.org/safeguarding-children/
18   http://www.bbc.co.uk/connect/needtoknow/safety_online
19   http://www.google.com/apps/intl/en/edu/#utm_medium=et&utm_source=catch_all
20   http://www.dropbox.com
21   http://drive.google.com/start
22   http://skydrive.com
23   https://www.icloud.com/

but if you want to be more public you can also post items on Facebook, Twitter!

The services that work like applications are interactive, unlike the old web pages that just showed a series of pictures or diagrams. These sites store the information you have added perhaps via a form and produce a new view on the web page such as a map that then links to a view of your house (Google Maps[24])– this whole section of the web page can be shared with others or added to another website. These 'mashups' where all sorts of web services can be linked altogether are part of the new scenery found on the internet.

The other useful thing about the storage that goes on with Cloud Computing is that items can be reached using any device that has a browser or app with a connection at any time – no longer do you need to decide which operating system or smart phone will work with the online services.

If you are using these services on your smartphone you may have already discovered that they know where you are – GPS with voice direction is also possible[25] and there is the ability to ask questions with Google Voice or Siri on the iPhone or iPad. These exciting services have meant that students are beginning to bring their own technology into schools – this has come to be known as BYOD (Bring your own device) when it is part of a school policy.

It can be very liberating for those who have specific learning difficulties including dyslexia, as a device that has been personalised using apps that help with reading and writing

---

24 https://maps.google.co.uk/
25 http://www.google.com/mobile/maps/

along with settings to suit individual needs can offer increased access to teaching and learning resources. The fact that the user has learnt how to use the device in their own time, usually results in an increased level of technological confidence that may not be found when having to use an organisation's technologies.

There are possible problems for those having to plan for the use of 'user owned' technologies and these have tended to come to the fore rather than the possible savings and access options. The sort of issues discussed include security of data, bullying online if users have not received sufficient training about e-safety, problems with storage of inappropriate data and hacking because there are so many apps that can be downloaded that expose the network to unauthorised access.

Finally when it comes to thinking 'What Next...?' one of the least tried and tested technologies are 'web apps' that are device and operating system independent. In other words these are apps that are developed to be used via a browser such as Safari, Opera, Chrome, Firefox and Internet Explorer so they will cross the Apple, Android and Windows operating systems. They work when you are connected to the web and tend to automatically adapt to suit the size of the screen you are using – so you may find a full page view on a tablet screen but a tab or linear view on a mobile phone. Marketplaces such as the OpenAppMkt for HTML5 mobile apps [26] are beginning to appear where downloads are directed to your device and the majority of the apps are free.

---

26 **http://openappmkt.com/**

It is hoped that problems that restrict access to the internet in teaching and learning environments and the use of personal devices can be overcome so a wider range of technologies can be used when appropriate allowing for a level of personalisation of learning that has not been achieved to-date.